Reflections on Classroom Thinking Strategies

Practical Strategies to Encourage Thinking in Your Classroom

(Sixth Edition)

Eric Frangenheim

P·C·P
Paul Chapman
Publishing

Paul Chapman Publishing
A SAGE Publications Company
1 Oliver's Yard
55 City Road
London EC1Y 1SP

SAGE Publications Inc
2455 Teller Road
Thousand Oaks, California 91320

SAGE Publications India Pvt Ltd
B-42, Panchsheel Enclave
Post Box 4109
New Delhi 110 017

Library of Congress Control Number available

A catalogue record for this book is available from the British Library

ISBN 1-4129-1828-6
ISBN 1-4129-1829-4 (pbk)

Typeset by Cheryll Beaumont
Printed on paper from sustainable resources
Printed in Great Britain by Cromwell Press Ltd, Trowbridge, Wilts

Contents

> This book is dedicated to a wonderful group of people
> – Terri, Dr Nichola, Frances, Julie, Jennie and Dr Mick.

Sixth Reflections – an Update

Thanks to SAGE Publications and Paul Chapman Publishing, this is the sixth printing of this book in its present shape. Despite some dreadful printing and binding, the first version sold out in under a year and thus I embarked on the present format. After four more editions and very encouraging sales to schools and universities in Australia and New Zealand, I was encouraged to approach Sage Publications in the UK in December 2004 and to my utter delight, they have taken on the world-wide printing and distribution rights (excluding Australia and New Zealand). This edition differs from the Australian 5th Edition in that I have removed certain material and replaced it with some more recent ideas forged in classrooms and workshops as well as the ideas from a good Brisbane friend, Gerard Alford (Judge–Jury, 3:2:1:RIQ and MASC).

I continue to travel through Australia and, apart from my home state, Queensland, have now added Victoria, West Australia, New South Wales, Northern Territory and New Zealand to my stamping ground, meeting wonderfully dedicated educators who have fun in their classrooms. More and more teachers tell me that thinking and learning strategies make a significant contribution to their personal practice. The advent of 'outcomes based learning' and 'productive pedagogies' makes the use of these strategies even more vital (see the poster at the foot of this page).

Since so many teachers are consciously planning and teaching with thinking strategies in mind, I have asked a few to contribute to this edition. Their ideas are to be found in the chapter 'Reflections from Other Classrooms' starting on page 95. I'm sure their reflections on their practice will assist many others in the quest to be 'an even better teacher'. In the past two years I have become more closely associated with Laurie Kelly of Mindworks. A former teacher, Laurie consults mainly to the corporate world and government departments. He has invited me to present workshops on 'Creating the Thinking Environment' and much of the material is the same as in my teacher sessions. It is quite exhilarating running these workshops with managers, trainers, facilitators and business owners as it underlines the universality of the application of these thinking tools as well as the importance of life long learning skills.

I do hope that this book and its many thinking strategies encourage all educators to create '**even better learning environments**'.

Eric Frangenheim   (June 2005)

N.B. The revised Bloom's Taxonomy is used throughout this edition. Please go to page 22 for an explanation.

Acknowledgments

I have collected and modified many strategies over the past twenty years and am unsure of the source of some. Several have been picked up at workshops on Gifted and Talented and others from those dealing with Effective Learning and Teaching. Presenters such as Joan Dalton and Tony Ryan promote these strategies. Many of these are present in a wide variety of books on thinking and teaching. I have attempted to discover the designers of these strategies and have, to the best of my knowledge, acknowledged them in the References List. The **Comma Thinking Rule**, **1:4:P:C:R**, **Think:Whisper:Repeat:Share** and **Extent Barometer** are my own design. I have also modified many of the strategies to suit my purpose.

Acknowledgment of people in my growth

Though I have been teaching since 1970, the years 1989–1992 were the most significant in my journey as a teacher/educator/facilitator. It was the period during which I was based at Rockhampton, Queensland, Australia, as Education Adviser for Gifted and Talented students in the Capricornia Region with Education Queensland. The Regional Director, the late Mike Maher, gave me *carte blanche* to develop the consultancy as I saw fit since there were few models to follow. Within that atmosphere of total professional trust and support, I felt both valued and fulfilled. More importantly, I was part of a team of ten regional consultants spread throughout this vast state led by the State Coordinator, Di Rankin. The team met for one week per year for our annual inservice and share fest. I learnt more about education from my colleagues in these four years than in my previous twenty years as a teacher and administrator and it convinced me to remain working at the classroom level.

I therefore wish to acknowledge the stimulus and growth I received from the likes of Ralph Pirozzo, Tony Ryan, Ros Roodveldt, Marg Usher, Jill Hole, Justina Crawford, Owen Langdale, Ross Craig, Karen Berghofer, Geoff Harper, Lyne Megarrity, Michelle Leben, Judith Bandidt, Carol Laherty, Denise Cox, Donna Bretherton and Marlene Eltham. It was from these colleagues, other education advisers in the Capricornia Region and the many classroom teachers and administrators with whom I had the privilege to work in that period, that I gained a deep passion for the power and importance of creating the Thinking Classroom, since all learners, no matter what their level of ability, benefit from a truly stimulating classroom which is offered day after day. I also gratefully acknowledge the work of Marion Mackenzie and the Queensland Association of Gifted and Talented Children.

Other people who have been an inspiration and who have shared their knowledge are the contributors to '*Reflections from Other Classrooms*' starting on page 95: Laurie Kelly, Dr John Hunt, Margaret Bishop, Kath Layton and Katherine Mian.

John O'Donahue, who challenged the way we did things.

Margaret Bishop of Bishop Education, who has encouraged me to put my ideas on paper and gently reminded me to get on with it. She has also generously given me her time and invaluable advise on the production side of publishing a book. Margaret has been a great supporter of the Xpata Lesson Planner.

Cheryll Beaumont, who has amazing ability to translate and decipher my ideas and who uses her wonderful creativity to make them fit for public consumption.

To all of the above, thank you for your sharing!

Copyright Acknowledgements

The Best Learning takes place when the Teacher is Quiet

This depends on:
1. a good question/activity
2. an appropriate strategy
3. a clear time frame

Introduction

The major purpose of this book is to introduce teachers (and by that I mean all types of teachers – classroom teachers, administrators, teacher aids, parents and coaches) to various individual and group thinking strategies related to specific questions and activities. This guide is a personal interpretation and critique of those strategies which I use frequently in my teaching or professional development sessions. I have strong personal anecdotal evidence to convince me that more learning takes place when I stop talking and allow and expect learners to be engaged in purposeful thinking and learning (see Wall Poster opposite).

All strategies presented in this book offer teachers the opportunity to have a break from active teaching and offer the students an opportunity to be independent learners. It is therefore an attempt to encourage the transfer of learning energy from behind the teacher's desk to the learners' side of the teacher's desk. (See Wall Poster *Transfer of Teaching/Learning Energy* page 121.)

Good thinking does not happen automatically. Prejudice is the alternative to thinking. I remember listening to an excellent speech at Alexandra High School in Pietermaritzburg, South Africa, in the late 1970s. The guest of honour, Dr Brian Stuckenberg, director of the Natal Museum in that town, said, "Prejudice is the lazy person's way of thinking." Lazy people avoid effort. Thinking takes effort. Therefore, it needs to be taught overtly and explicitly, practised regularly and recognised, encouraged and praised whenever it occurs. The language of thinking needs to be used as part of the classroom interaction amongst all learners. The names of strategies and their rules could be displayed on the walls and from ceilings. (See Wall Posters) A basic knowledge of the six levels of Bloom's Taxonomy on page 122 (a framework for understanding and processing material at a cognitive level) is also important and learners should be able to identify any cognitive challenge and activity in terms of these six levels. (See Wall Poster *Learners are Empowered when...* overleaf.) A basic understanding of Gardner's Multiple Intelligence Model could also be shared with students.

Please refer to page *9*, '***Some Strategies for Thinking at Different Levels***'. This aims to link specific thinking strategies (Column headed 'Some Thinking Strategies') to the various levels of Bloom's Taxonomy. I do not believe it is particularly fair to expect students to analyse, hypothesise and be creative and evaluate if I do not offer them a strategy to do so. Offering students a **PCQ** or **Y Chart** will help them analyse (discuss or think about) far more successfully than simply relying on their innate ability or at worse, relying on the strategy of osmosis to bring success. Similarly, offering a **Scamper** or **Word Association** will help students be more creative and the **Decision-Making Matrix** will result in more effective evaluation.

I believe that the more we teach students a variety of thinking strategies and also teach them as tools to deal with specific levels of Bloom's Taxonomy, the more we will empower these students to become independent learners who can transfer learning and thinking strategies to other aspects of their lives and learning.

Advice to teachers

"Teach every child with passion, energy, creativity as if she/he would one day become a Mother Theresa, a Thomas Edison, Madame Curie, William Shakespeare, Tiger Woods, Mahatma Ghandi, Nelson Mandela, Nigel Kennedy, Bertrand Russell, a useful member of society – or as if he or she were your own child."

The renowned educationist, Prof Kapinsky P Frugenburger

Learners are Empowered When They

1. **understand the Level of the Question (Bloom)**

2. **understand the Expected Outcome**

3. **know which appropriate strategy/tool to employ**

This book does not deal with every strategy listed on the page entitled '*Some Strategies for Thinking at Different Levels*'. Rather, it covers those strategies which I use most frequently in my classroom practice. I do not cover most of the strategies linked to the three lower levels of Bloom's Taxonomy of the Cognitive domain since the vast majority of teachers regularly employ strategies to help students know, understand and use. This book deals with strategies to assist with Analysing, Evaluating and Creating since I am acutely conscious that for too many years as a teacher of history, I had no specific strategies to help my students operate at these levels, apart from the 'strategy' of osmosis and their own natural ability.

I hope that by incorporating these strategies in your curriculum unit planning (if they are new to you), you will enhance your classroom practice and increasingly stimulate the learning environment which is so vital to learning with a purpose.

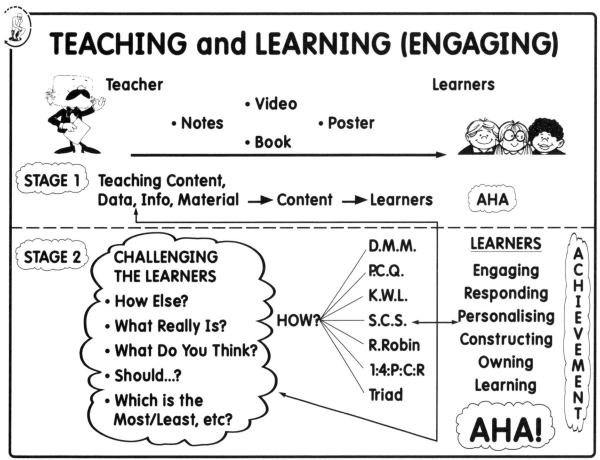

Eric Frangenheim, Rodin Educational Consultancy ©

This book encourages the use of Stage 2 after Stage 1, since using appropriate thinking strategies for certain questions will lead to the benefits listed in the graphic above.

ENJOY CREATING THE THINKING CLASSROOM

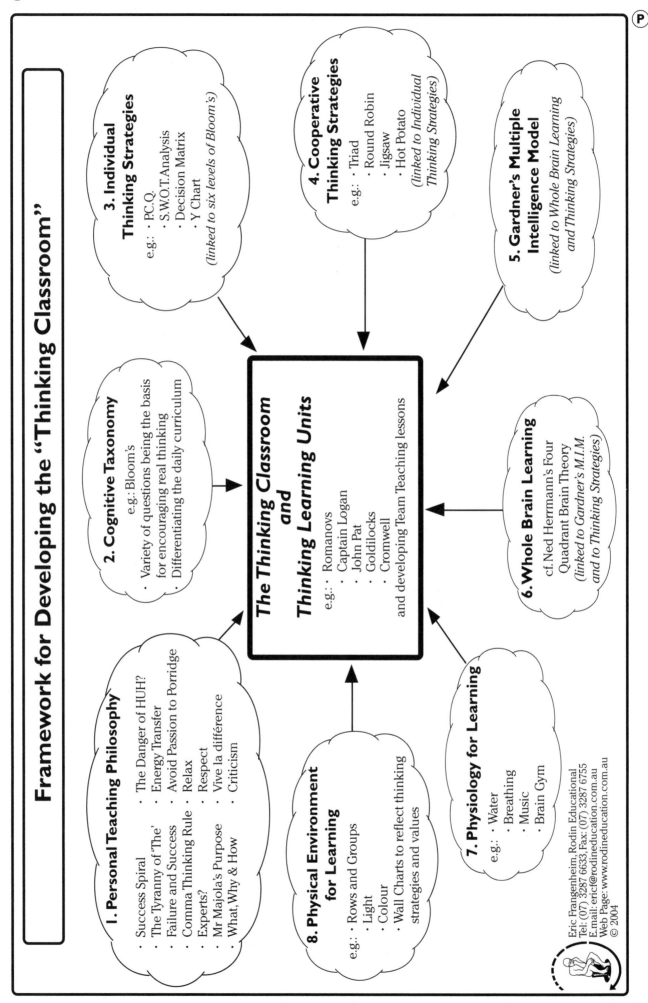

Framework for Developing the "Thinking Classroom"

3. Individual Thinking Strategies

e.g.:
· PC.Q.
· S.W.O.T. Analysis
· Decision Matrix
· Y Chart

(linked to six levels of Bloom's)

4. Cooperative Thinking Strategies

e.g.:
· Triad
· Round Robin
· Jigsaw
· Hot Potato

(linked to Individual Thinking Strategies)

5. Gardner's Multiple Intelligence Model

(linked to Whole Brain Learning and Thinking Strategies)

2. Cognitive Taxonomy

e.g.: Bloom's
· Variety of questions being the basis for encouraging real thinking
· Differentiating the daily curriculum

The Thinking Classroom and Thinking Learning Units

e.g.:
· Romanovs
· Captain Logan
· John Pat
· Goldilocks
· Cromwell

and developing Team Teaching lessons

6. Whole Brain Learning

cf. Ned Herrmann's Four Quadrant Brain Theory

(linked to Gardner's M.I.M. and to Thinking Strategies)

1. Personal Teaching Philosophy

· Success Spiral
· The Tyranny of 'The'
· Failure and Success
· Comma Thinking Rule
· Experts?
· Mr Majola's Purpose
· What, Why & How
· The Danger of HUH?
· Energy Transfer
· Avoid Passion to Porridge
· Relax
· Respect
· Vive la différence
· Criticism

8. Physical Environment for Learning

e.g.:
· Rows and Groups
· Light
· Colour
· Wall Charts to reflect thinking strategies and values

7. Physiology for Learning

e.g.:
· Water
· Breathing
· Music
· Brain Gym

Eric Frangenheim, Rodin Educational
Tel: (07) 3287 6633, Fax: (07) 3287 6755
E. mail: ericf@rodineducation.com.au
Web Page: www.rodineducation.com.au
© 2004

Some Strategies for Thinking at Different Levels

4. Some Cooperative and Collaborative Strategies (HOW)

- 1:2:4
- 1:3:Share
- 1:3:6:Share
- 1:4:P:C:R
- 3:2:1:RIQ
- Assigning Roles
- Hot Potato
- Jigsaw
- Numbered Heads
- Round Robin
- Setting Group Goals
- Silent Card Shuffle
- Think, Pair, Share
- TRIAD

5. Howard Gardner's Multiple Intelligence Model (WHO)

- Verbal Linguistic (*Word Smart*)
- Logical Mathematical (*Number Smart*)
- Visual/Spatial (*Picture Smart*)
- Body/Kinesthetic (*Body Smart*)
- Musical/Rhythmic (*Music Smart*)
- Interpersonal (*People Smart*)
- Intrapersonal (*Self Smart*)
- Naturalistic (*Seeing Connections*)

© 2005

1. Some Thinking Skills (WHAT)	2. Bloom (WHY)	3. Some Thinking Strategies (HOW)
Complexity, Designing, Elaborating, Extrapolating, Flexibility, Forecasting, Formulating, Hypothesising, Modifying, Organising, Originality, Planning, Proposing, Risk-taking, Synthesising	Create	1:4:P:C:R, AGO, Brick Wall Key, Combinations Key, Construction Key, CPS, Disadvantages/Improvements T, Forced Relationships, Pros:Cons:Improve, Random Input, MASC, Scamper, "So what is the Problem?", The Ridiculous Key, TWERP, Variations Key, What If Key, Y Chart
Arguing, Assessing, Choosing, Concluding, Deciding, Determining, Judging, Justifying, Prioritising, Rating, Recommending, Selecting, Verifying	Evaluate	3:2:1:RIQ, Advantages/Disadvantages T, Decision Making Matrix, Disadvantages/Improvements T, Extent Barometer, Judge Jury, Pros:Cons:Improve, PCQ, Relevant/Irrelevant T, Reliable/Unreliable T, Tournament Prioritising, Y Chart
Arguing, Analysing, Categorising, Comparing, Complex Thinking, Differentiating, Summarising, Contrasting, Debating, Deducing, Deeper Thinking, Investigating, Separating, Discussing, Distinguishing, Examining, Explaining, Identifying	Analyse	3:2:1:RIQ, Attribute Grouping, Brainstorming, Commonalities Key, CPS, Decision Making Matrix, Different Uses Key, Disadvantages/Improvements T, Fact/Opinion T, Five Whys?, Good/Poor Reasoning T, Judge Jury, KWL, Mind Map, Picture Key, Pros:Cons:Improve, PCQ, Ridiculous Statement, S.W.O.T. Analysis, Silent Card Shuffle, T Charts, The Interpretation Key, Y Chart, 5W&1H
Applying, Calculating, Compiling, Completing, Constructing, Demonstrating, Extrapolating, Illustrating, Inferring, Showing, Solving, Using	Apply	Brainstorming, CPS, Different Uses Key, Flow Chart, Graphic Organiser, Reverse Listing Key, Silent Card Shuffle
Describing, Explaining, Interpreting, Outlining, Paraphrasing, Restating, Simple Summary, Translating, Understanding	Understand	AGO, Brick Wall Key, Generalisations, Graphic Organisers, Metaphor, Mind Map, Multiple Intelligence Model, PCQ, Reverse Listing, Silent Card Shuffle, Visualisation, Visuals, Word Summary
Defining, Fluency, Knowing, Labelling, Listing, Locating, Memorising, Naming, Remembering, Retelling, Stating	Remember	Acronyms, Acrostics, Answer-Question Key, Attribute Listing, Brainstorming, Different Uses Key, KWL, Mnemonics, See-Saw, Silent Card Shuffle, What If

Eric Frangenheim
Rodin Educational Consultancy   Ph: (07) 3287 6633
PO Box 3369, Loganholme, Qld 4129   Fax: (07) 3287 6755
email: ericf@rodineducation.com.au
Web: www.rodineducation.com.au

Tony Ryan – Thinkers Keys and Mindlinks
John Langhrer – Teaching Thinking Strategies
Joan Dalton's Workshops
Thomas Armstrong – "Multiple Intelligences in the Classroom" 1994

Reflections on Classroom Thinking Strategies

(P)

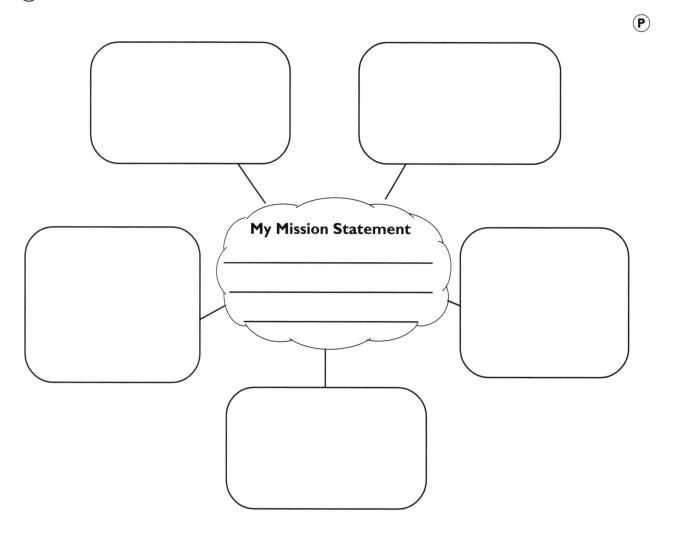

My Mission Statement
_____
_____
_____

from
Passion to Passion
or
from
Passion to Porridge

Eric Frangenheim, Rodin Educational Consultancy ©

This is an
"EXPERT-FREE ZONE"

Eric Frangenheim, Rodin Educational Consultancy ©

p.10

Eric Frangenheim ©

Personal Teaching Philosophy

All of us have a belief system or an informal and formal philosophy, some of which are dynamic and empowering and some of which are limiting. It may be useful for teachers to be aware of their own beliefs and philosophies in terms of teaching, learning and thinking and then promote those beliefs which enhance the educative process. The concept map opposite may provide an opportunity to articulate some of your beliefs. Develop this as you apply the ideas in this book.

I have tried to isolate those beliefs which I think are important and promote them in teaching situations. They are all connected in some manner to my mission statement of 'Promoting Thinking in Learning'. These beliefs are to be found on the page *Framework for Developing the Thinking Classroom* on page 8.

Some of these beliefs have their own chapter following this page whilst the others are explained here briefly.

The Tyranny of THE

In 1989, at the World Conference on Gifted and Talented Students in Sydney, I listened to Paul McCready, the inventor of the man-propelled aircraft, *The Gossamer Albatross*. He said that many people are limited by the 'Tyranny of THE' and by that he meant that too often we look for one answer, 'the' answer. He explained that this resulted in orthodoxy, conventionality, safety, a limited imagination, and impoverished problem solving. He encouraged teachers to get away from the 'Tyranny of THE' by asking questions such as "what are all the answers to …" and "how many different ways…" instead of "what is **the** answer" and "what is **the** way". From this I have developed *The Comma Thinking Rule* on page 29.

Avoid Passion to Porridge

I have always been impressed by those experienced teachers, educational leaders, school administrators and heads of departments who nurture and encourage those teachers who enter schools with a passion for teaching and ensure that the flame of passion never dies. The same holds true for those teachers who ensure that their students maintain a love for learning. Conversely, I am highly unimpressed by people who use a relentless cynicism to affect some teachers so that their passion turns to a 'porridge-type' performance. Unfortunately we also find that many students have become cynical about learning and have lost that early quality of curiosity which characterises young children. I am impressed by those schools where leaders and teachers are all pushing the same message of personal excellence, persistence and the benefits of a good education. Leadership is exactly that – it is letting everyone know that what we are doing in our schools is important.

If all teachers were to treat their classroom as if it were their own business, say a corner shop, then passion for what they are doing would be the least that their clients would expect. We can no longer expect students to be docile Pavlovian learners. They expect to be impressed and motivated by teachers who believe absolutely in **their** business of education!

Experts

See graphic on left. To encourage students to become risk takers, I do the following. I ask them to point to themselves and say "I am not an expert". Some of the students find this a bit difficult but they warm to the idea when I invite them to point at their peers and say "You are not an expert". This external assessment they seem to find very easy! I then ask them to point at me and say "He is not an expert either". I then explain that since we have established an Expert-Free Zone, they are no longer to worry about being wrong and can now concentrate on the business of learning which has to be accompanied by mistakes. I also make it clear that a thinking environment demands total respect for the feelings of others and that destroying or damaging the self-esteem of others is basically criminal since it suffocates and prevents good learning.

Paradigm Shift

T. Edison

9,999/10,000

"I worked out 9,999 ways how NOT to make a Light Bulb"

Failure

The only failures are those who never TRY.

(agree, disagree, suggest, contribute, etc)

Those who do try simply experience differing degrees of success.

100

50

0

Failure and Success

See graphics on left. I was always impressed by teachers who encourage students to be risk-takers and who would then debrief any resulting mistakes. I am also aware that a classroom or learning environment which discourages risk-taking and promotes the intellectual control and superiority of the teacher or facilitator is unlikely to encourage lateral thinkers. For these and other reasons, I discuss the idea that the only failures are those who do not contribute in the classroom. Sometimes we are totally wrong, sometimes totally right, but usually we are somewhere in between. I explain that I respect those who TRY! I also encourage them to think of the attitude of Thomas Edison who saw his experiments as learning opportunities. In fact, one of the reasons I was keen to migrate to Australia was the refreshing attitude of "Give it a go!"

Paradigm Shift

The story of Edison's invention of the light bulb is inspirational, not only for its effects on the world and for his persistence, but even more so for his view or paradigm about the process. I encourage learners to be inspired by his commitment and for his view on those 9,999 experiments which did not result in success. He saw things differently and so should all of us. Is our drink half full or half empty, our holidays half gone or half to go? Are we being forced out of our comfort zone or into our excitement and growth zone? Ask students to generate a list of negative and positive paradigm reflections or circumstances.

Relax

We only have one life on earth, so let us relax and enjoy ourselves as much as possible. Though we need to be serious about what we do, we could encourage more laughter in our classroom and not take things too seriously. By this I mean keeping things in perspective. In August 1997 I listened to Bill Rogers in Emerald in Queensland. He displayed one of Leunig's cartoons which showed a gentleman concentrating on a small dark dot on a large white sheet. The message was clear. Don't concentrate on the negatives (the spot) in life when most of what we experience is positive (the unmarked area).

Respect and 'Vive la Difference'

A basis for the thinking classroom is that we welcome diversity, difference and ambiguity. We learn to suspend judgment until we have applied some clear thinking procedures. We learn to delay gratification, pause before we respond and look for the other point of view. We need to appreciate that untold hurt is caused in the name of so-called evaluation or decision making. It is too easy to pass judgment on another person or dismiss the worth of an institution, event or proposal. Good thinkers are fair thinkers because they are taught that facts, information and data need to be brought to the fore and used in an analysis situation to give structure and clarity to the information before any evaluation is made. In this way, a great deal of unnecessary hurt will be avoided and more people will think more honestly and productively.

The following chapters refer to items dealing with Personal Teaching Philosophy:
- **Mr Majola and SUE**
- **The Success Spiral**
- **The 'What', 'Why' and 'How' of Teaching and Learning**
- **Brainstorming**
- **The Comma Thinking Rule**
- **The Danger of HUH?**
- **Personal Criticism**

P

Mr Majola's Question and S.U.E.

Shut Up Eric

S.U.E.1
- Why is this useful?
- How did it promote learning?
etc

S.U.E.2
- Where can I specifically use this?

Mr Majola's Question and SUE
(A call for reflection and transfer)

In the 1970s I was a volunteer lecturer at an informal teacher training college in Pietermaritzburg, Kwa Zulu-Natal, in South Africa. We met after school two afternoons per week for two years. I had about sixty teachers, mainly Zulu, who were upgrading their qualifications. Lecture notes were supplied and I was one of the presenters or lecturers. I will never forget this fulfilling experience but I particularly remember one question asked by Mr Majola, a school principal. It happened when I was explaining a section on the Balkan crisis leading up to the outbreak of World War One. It was tedious material which I presented in a tedious manner when Mr Majola caught my attention and said "Excuse me. Why are we learning this?" It was a fair question aimed as much at my lacklustre delivery as to the lack of relevance to their experience. My immediate and only answer was "Because it is in the syllabus" but the question spurred me to examine why I did things and to look for purpose and to share this purpose with my students in order to motivate them more.

Then in 1990 I attended a workshop at Moura State high School one Sunday presented by the inspirational Dr John Edwards, at that stage a lecturer at James Cook University. Apart from warning teachers to avoid delivering a 'Sea of Blahs' at our students (at which I was particularly adept), he also talked about the importance of offering 'Perception Checks' to our students on a regular basis. I have taken Mr Majola's question and Dr John Edward's suggestion seriously and amalgamated them into my learning framework and have come up with my most important strategy, **SUE** which is an acronym for ***Shut Up Eric***. I regularly employ this strategy in my workshops with teachers and parents as well as in my classroom.

SUE has two parts

SUE 1 asks workshop participants to reflect on

- what was useful about what they have just learnt?
- how it promoted learning and satisfied styles of learning?
- how it would complement their own classroom practice?
- and how it would make their classroom EVEN BETTER?

SUE 1 asks students questions such as

- What is the main point being made here?
- What is interesting about this?
- How can I use this information or strategy elsewhere in this course, in other subjects, in my life?
- What did **you** like or not like about this strategy or information?

SUE 2 asks workshop participants to decide

- where they could specifically employ each strategy or idea in their daily teaching?
- when they will employ or apply this strategy next?

SUE 2 asks students

- What they could do differently next time now that they have a new strategy or now that they have this piece of information?

Reflection and Transfer

🤔 SUE 1

What is good about this strategy?
How could it promote learning and thinking?

_____
_____
_____
_____
_____
_____
_____
_____
_____

🤔 SUE 2   *Where can I use this?*

Class: _____

Topic: _____

How?: _____
_____
_____
_____

🤔 SUE 2   *Where can I use this?*

Class: _____

Topic: _____

How?: _____
_____
_____
_____

Name of Strategy

_____
_____

🤔 SUE 1

How can I modify this strategy to suit my style?

_____
_____
_____
_____
_____
_____
_____

🤔 SUE 2   *Where can I use this?*

Class: _____

Topic: _____

How?: _____
_____
_____

🤔 SUE 2   *Where can I use this?*

Class: _____

Topic: _____

How?: _____
_____
_____

🤔 SUE 1

Where else outside my main practice can I use this?

_____
_____
_____
_____
_____
_____

🤔 SUE 2   *Where can I use this?*

Class: _____

Topic: _____

How?: _____

These are some of the reasons why I use **SUE** in my teacher and parent workshops and in my classroom:

- it gives learners a break from my voice
- it places responsibility on the learners to react to what they have learnt
- it allows learners to make personal connections
- it sends a clear message that learning is a two-way street
- most importantly, it transfers energy to the other side of the desk (see p.121)
- it constantly reminds me of the importance of relevance, transfer and purpose.

This is what Mr Majola, with the clear common sense of a perceptive learner, was asking me all those years ago. He of course, has no idea the effect he has had on me as an educator, and I thank him in his absence!

The use of SUE in this book

One of the truths about learners is that they need to be motivated to learn. One way to motivate people is to allow them to realise that something they are learning is valuable and has a purpose and a benefit. For this reason, asking learners to reflect on SUE 2 is more likely to lead to growth in their personal practice and therefore is more likely to motivate them to learn. It is for this reason that I offer a reflection sheet opposite most strategies presented in this book, space permitting. Please take the time to answer both SUE 1 and SUE 2. Remember – you are in charge of your learning, and since learning is a dynamic process, act upon it.

THE SUCCESS SPIRAL

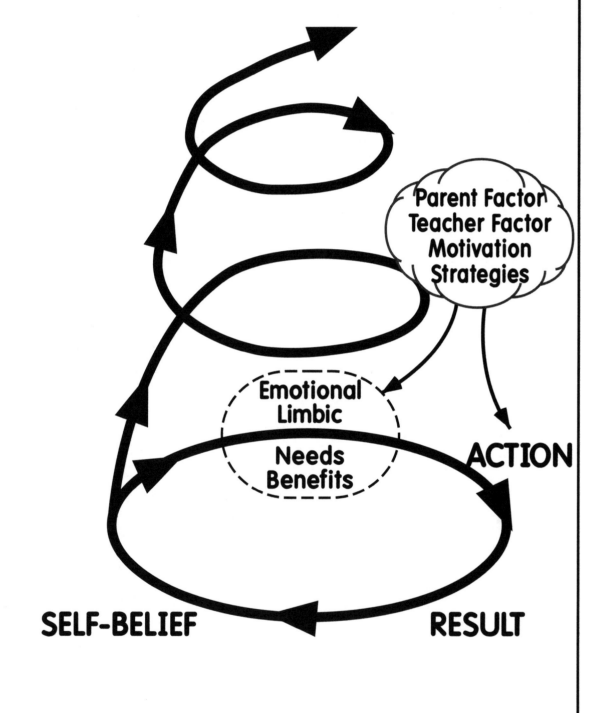

Parent Factor
Teacher Factor
Motivation
Strategies

Emotional
Limbic

Needs
Benefits

ACTION

SELF-BELIEF

RESULT

Adapted from Stephanie Burns, Learning to Learn Workshop 1993

Eric Frangenheim, Rodin Educational Consultancy ©

The Success Spiral

In 1974, one of my friends, Shirley Schoerie, asked me what I taught. I replied "History". She responded by saying that she taught "students" and I quickly thought that she was being a smart-alec.

However, over the years I realised that she was quite correct – I am teaching students, not history. In 1993, I attended an intensive two and a half day Learning to Learn workshop in Brisbane facilitated by Stephanie Burns and came across the Success Spiral, which is central to our practice as educators.

Stephanie explained that all learners have *Potential*, and that the trick is to place learners in situations so that when they take *Action* (try it), the *Result* is successful, leading to positive talk and positive *Self-belief*. This in turn leads to a belief that one has *Potential*, to learn more, take more *Action*, experience a successful *Result*, have greater *Self-belief* and continue in this positive cycle leading to the Success Spiral.

Going back to my friend's comment about teaching students and with what I have learnt about the human brain and motivation, I have added the Limbic-Emotional to the diagram. It is extremely difficult to teach someone who sees no need in the lesson and so before we engage the cognitive processes, we need to engage the emotions (found in the Limbic system of the brain). We need to motivate, give purpose to our lessons, explain benefits of the learning and display passion and excitement as often as possible.

 It is then that we can start the cognitive side of the lesson, leading to student response (Action) which presumably will lead to a successful Result and a positive Self-belief. The cycle will be repeated and repeated, resulting in more complex learning and even more satisfying feelings of self-worth. Eventually the stage of Unconscious Competence is reached – the goal for both teacher and learner. This is the upwards Success Spiral.

The opposite is also true. The more we have negative results, the more our self-esteem suffers, the more we doubt our potential, and so on until we spiral downwards.

I point out to students/learners that they have a huge responsibility in this process. Teachers are not magicians, and if both parties have a positive attitude, the *Success Spiral* is almost guaranteed.

After all, learning is a partnership – it is a two-way street!!

Effective Thinkers and Learners

- 💡 **Pause before they answer**
- 💡 **Give reasons for their answers**
- 💡 **See criticism as information**
- 💡 **Are relaxed about making mistakes**
- 💡 **Are not afraid to experiment**
- 💡 **Always try to see the other points of view**
- 💡 **Show humility**
- 💡 **Are good listeners**

Eric Frangenheim, Rodin Educational Consultancy ©

Ⓟ

TEACHING & LEARNING

WHAT? → Content

→ Questions/Activities

WHY? → Assessment Purposes
Learning Outcomes

→ *Transfer and Link to other
- Topics
- Subjects
- Life

* As part of the process —>
objective/goal e.g., essay/poem

- Motivation
- Purpose

HOW? → Teacher Exposition
Ⓐ and Worksheets

Ⓑ

- Student Involvement

- Transfer of Energy

	Thinking Strategies	Content Transfer via Ⓐ plus
• Create		
• Evaluate		
• Analyse	**KWL**	• Stimulus
• Apply	**DMM**	
• Understand		
• Remember		
Group Strategies **ROUND ROBIN**		e.g.: Video Articles Stories etc

The What, Why and How of Teaching and Learning

If you had asked me some years ago **What** I was teaching to my Year 10 class, I may have answered "The French Revolution" (the content) – a fair answer.

If you then asked me **Why** I was teaching that, I may have answered "Because it is in the syllabus and will soon be tested" – also a fair answer.

If you had then followed up those two questions with **How** I was teaching the French Revolution, I would probably have answered "through the use of up-front teaching, notes or hand-outs, maps, a few pictures and some worksheets" or, what certain unkind but truthful observers would sometimes call, 'shut up sheets'.

I taught this way very successfully (sic?) for many years and, on reflection, this was clearly a solid **teaching paradigm**.

However, over the past 15 years or so, like many others, I have been exposed to some wonderful educators who have taken me out of my **comfort zone** and into an **excitement** and **growth zone**. I have always claimed that I was a teacher of thinking and that I used my subject, history, as the vehicle to encourage my students to think. I now realise that I had only gone part of the way to making them think. I kept control, I did the talking, I did the thinking, I displayed and explained the critical analysis and the students simply remembered much, most or all of it and with Pavlovian obedience served it back to me. The real tragedy is that not only did **I** think they were thinking, **they** thought they were thinking. Though my intentions were clear, they were not effective because I lacked a real understanding or an educational framework on which to create the thinking classroom.

I now consider the **What** in teaching to be the questions and activities which I present to my students as part of the lesson plan. If there are five questions and activities for the lesson, then those are the **What**. I am therefore concentrating on what is being **learnt** by the students rather than what I am **teaching**.

Because I know the importance of **motivating** learners, I also spend some time persuading my students about relevance and importance of what they are learning. This is the **Why** of the lesson activities. I will explain the purpose of each activity in terms of the contribution to the outcome. If it has no purpose, it should possibly not be in the lesson. I explain that a certain activity or question is important as part of the process of completing the unit. I also offer reflection (SUE 1 – p.15) opportunities so that learners can make connections between the **What** we are learning and other topics with which we have dealt in the past, with other subjects they are learning at school and to decide if there is any link between the material and events in their daily life and the world at large. This is, of course, Mr Majola's influence. I want to avoid situations where my students are thinking or asking "Why are we learning this?" and seeing or sensing no relevance or purpose.

However, the most important part of the learning environment is the **How** of the lesson. Once I know **What** I want my students to achieve and the **Why**, I then apply the **How** question.

I try to ensure that this is the most important part of my lesson planning. I use the page entitled *'Some Strategies for Thinking at Different Levels'* (page 9) and select questions or activities from the first column 'Some Thinking Skills'. By varying the cognitive level in terms of Bloom's Taxonomy, I am differentiating the daily curriculum, offering a variety of cognitive challenges and am more likely to extend all students. With most questions I select an appropriate Thinking Strategy from the middle column. For example, I may employ a PCQ (Pros, Cons, Questions) if I am asking an Analysis or Evaluation question. Because I have a great admiration for cooperative learning, I will regularly employ one of these strategies, such as a Round Robin or Think: Pair: Share, from the Cooperative Strategies box. This can be done in conjunction with a PCQ so that the synergy of the class is employed instead of relying on individual performance. In this case, we are using a group strategy (Round Robin – the **How**) and a specific thinking strategy (PCQ – the **How**) in order to handle an Analysis or Evaluation activity (the **What**).

Another part of the **How** is to ensure that the Multiple Intelligence Model (Howard Gardner) has a role in lesson planning. I am referring to the Left and Right Brain box on the Teaching and Learning sheet (p.20) and the bottom right box on the sheet titled *'Some Strategies for Thinking at Different Levels'* (p.9).

The *'Framework for Developing the Thinking Classroom'* is an overview of my views on Teaching and Learning. This book will deal largely with 1. Personal Teaching Philosophy, 2. Cognitive Taxonomy, 3. Individual Thinking Strategies, 4. Cooperative Thinking Strategies, and incidentally with 5. Gardner's Multiple Intelligence Model and 6. Whole Brain Learning. Numbers 7 and 8, those dealing with Physiology of Learning and Physical Environment for learning, are not covered in this book.

Please refer to the Lesson Plan on 'The Sinking of The Titanic' on the next four (4) pages. This lesson plan is an example of the *What, Why and How of Teaching and Learning* in practice.

The Revised Bloom's Taxonomy

The cognitive taxonomy developed by Benjamin Bloom in the 1950s has proved to be an invaluable tool for teachers. It provides a clear guide to levels of thinking and the processing of learning experiences. As with any effective framework, reappraisal can lead to modification.

Lorin Anderson, a former student of Benjamin Bloom, and a team of cognitive psychologists has made various suggestions for dynamic reappraisal of the Taxonomy.

Firstly, the categories have changed from nouns to verbs. Learning is an active experience, and to make use of these verbs is a positive step. The categories have been changed as follows:
- Knowledge to Remember
- Comprehension to Understand
- Application to Apply
- Analysis to Analyse
- Synthesis to Create
- Evaluation to Evaluate

In addition, Anderson argues that in terms of a hierarchy, **Evaluate** precedes **Create**, and therefore these two swap around. However, it is not always necessary to view the higher order cognitive levels as a hierarchy. In constructing a set of learning experiences, whether it is a single lesson, a lesson as part of a series of lessons, or when constructing a unit of work, it is important to 'start with the outcome in mind'.

If one wants a discussion or an investigation (**Analyse**), then it is natural that the learner will also **Evaluate** existing structures and **Create** new ideas. However, the main focus is on analysing the topic.

If the major focus is to pass judgement, such as in deciding whether an action was appropriate or not (**Evaluate**), then it is natural that the learner will **Analyse** the matter and come up with alternative ideas or actions (**Create**) before focusing on a decision.

If on the other hand, the main focus is to **Create**, such as in proposing a solution to a problem, then it is natural for the learner to **Analyse** the present situation under discussion and make decisions (**Evaluate**) before generating solutions to the problem.

Whatever the task, the teacher will assess the student on the major outcome. Other aspects of the taxonomy, including the foundation thinking (often referred to as lower order thinking) will be employed as well.

In conclusion, the way I see the taxonomy is that at the base are the three foundation levels of **Remember**, **Understand** and **Apply**. Above that are the three higher order levels of **Analyse**, **Evaluate** and **Create**. These too can be visualised or organised as a hierarchy, or can be seen as three rotating spheres, interacting with each other, but with one of them being the primary focus for a learning outcome.

Lesson Plan

As a consultant working with teachers and students, I concentrate a great deal on the coaching model whereby I work with teachers who share their lesson plan and lesson objectives with me. I then make a few suggestions based on the page, *'Some Strategies for Thinking at Different Levels'* and modify the lesson plan. The teacher and I also negotiate what each of us will be doing in that lesson.

What follows is a whole day lesson taught with two teachers, Penny Parker and John Lanau and their sixty Year 6 students at Macgregor State School, Brisbane. It was a wonderful lesson which far exceeded our expectations. The teachers were well prepared and had selected very effective and stimulating resources which kept the students at a high level of thinking and participation from 9.00am till 3.00pm. You will notice my name with John and Penny's. This simply indicates who taught which sections during the day.

I particularly wish to draw your attention to the terms What, Purpose and How. Referring to my chapter on the *What, Why and How of Teaching and Learning*, the lesson plan developed by the three of us distinguished between the What, that is the actual questions and activities, the Why or explaining the purpose of what the students have to do and the How, which is the strategy used to achieve the What.

The letters in brackets, next to each activity, refer to the level/s of Bloom's Taxonomy.

John Lanau and Penny Parker
Year 6 Teaching Partners

Why Did the Titanic Sink?

Macgregor State School
Lesson Plan

Requirements	• Little prior knowledge
Resources	• felt pens 3x8 cards – facts computer paper Epidiascope Mariner Music and CD TV and video player
Objectives	• Mystery angle • To write an explanatory text of the Sinking of the Titanic

---

Activity 1 — List of mysteries
(R&U)

Students • to offer the names of mysteries in history and life
(e.g., UFO, Bermuda Triangle, Love)

 Noisy Round Robin (p.82)

Teacher • Write 1 or 2 answers from each group of 4 on blackboard

Activity 2 — What are all the components of a mystery
(or reasons why they become mysteries) *(R&U)*

Purpose • To incorporate some of these features into the eventual explanatory text

 Silent Round Robin (p.83) John

Teacher • to debrief — link some of these components to what happened with the Titanic
(best 3 on blackboard)

Activity 3 — Focus on the Titanic

 Video

Purpose • Focus and gain knowledge of the events

 Eric

 Pairs (p.94)

6 x Human Causes	4 x Mechanical/Technical Causes
•	•
•	•
3 x Natural Causes	**2 x Cover Ups**
•	•
•	•
•	

Activity 4 — Understanding Strengths and Weaknesses of the Titanic

Purpose • Listening skills and deeper understanding of the situation

 T Chart (pp. 58 & 64)
Penny and John, as a duet, take it in turns to read short passages or offer pieces of information — 20 second pause after each

Students • to use this time to discuss and record the information either as *Strength* or *Weakness*

(A4 Sheet)

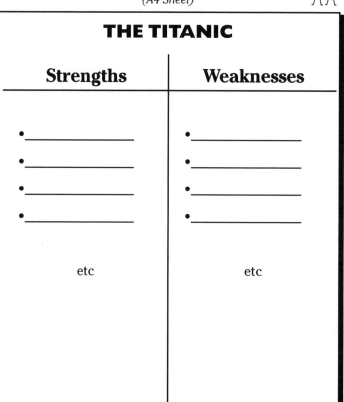

THE TITANIC

Strengths	Weaknesses
•_____	•_____
•_____	•_____
•_____	•_____
•_____	•_____
etc	etc

Activity 5 — Gain a more personal insight into the tragedy *(An)*

Purpose • To build up a data bank of information, opinions, feelings, etc which allows students to write their eventual explanatory text

 Y-Chart Analysis (p.47)

THE TITANIC TRAGEDY
Looks Like
· *class distinction*

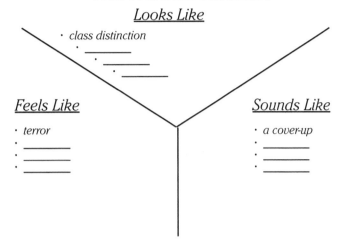

Feels Like
· *terror*

Sounds Like
· *a cover-up*

Activity 6 — Visual Stimulation *(Cr)*

 John and Penny discuss more features about:

a) the Titanic — using epidiascope (withdrawal room)

b) *Students* then are asked "How many questions can you ask about the events?" — using a Round Robin (noisy)

Teacher • Collate these on the board (best questions from each group)
Can this be used in Explanatory Text?

Activity 7 — Small group discussion *(R&U)*

Teacher to model • John to supply each group of 4 *(Students)* with a set of fact cards.

At random, each group turns over a card and discusses the information or picture.

Do the same for all 24 cards

Purpose • Preparation for the explanatory text

Activity 8 — Writing a Headline of the Sinking of the Titanic

(Cr)

Penny

1. *Teachers* give criteria for Headings —> on board via *students*

2. *Students* use

   - **Strengths | Weaknesses**

   - Y **Chart**

   - **Components**

   - **Cards**

   - **Lecturette Visuals**

   - **Questions**

Eric

3. Each group of four to use the **1:4:P:C:R** (p.91) – then write one headline

   larger paper

   Place on walls — Circulate — Refine

Then • Same process for Activity 9 (not part 3)

Activity 9 — Writing an Explanatory Text on the Tragedy

(Cr)

1. *Teachers* give criteria for Explanatory Text

2. *Students* use

   - **Components**   John

   - Y **Chart**

   - **Strengths | Weaknesses**

   - **Cards**

   - **Lecturette Visuals**

   - **Questions**

Activity 10 — Board of Enquiry

(Ev)

Brainstorming

Brainstorming is possibly the most common thinking strategy used in the classroom, enabling teachers to send clear messages that students' ideas and input are valued.

It is the cornerstone of the risk-taking and creative and critical classroom.

The basic rules to consider are:

1. Accept all ideas.

2. Do not be judgmental of any ideas and do not ask anyone to explain or defend/clarify their contribution.

3. Record all ideas, thereby giving equal worth to each idea and honouring the thinker.

4. Encourage the crazy ideas. Ask "What do you think John Cleese or Mr Bean would think of?"

5. Encourage students to build on top of other people's ideas (piggy backing).

6. Go for quantity and not for quality.

Reservations

I use whole-class brainstorming fairly sparingly for the reasons listed below.

1. Though the intention is to involve all students in the thinking process, I have found that many students move into the slip-stream of brighter or more creative students, and thus find this a useful opportunity to relax and switch off.

2. Dominant personalities sometimes take over, despite attempts by the teacher to encourage responses from a wide range of students.

3. Shy students, or those with brittle self-esteem, may feel threatened and vulnerable. Despite the ground rules which say that all ideas are of equal worth at first, many students tend to be over-critical of their own efforts.

4. In a class of thirty students, only 3% are actually active at any one moment when a teacher is conducting a brain storm session. If one takes into account the fact that student replies are often inaudible, forcing the teacher to repeat the answer for the benefit of the rest of the students, then the brainstorm session is indeed a most inefficient use of time!

Observation

I prefer to use a Round Robin or Hot Potato. Both are to be found in this book. There are other more efficient ways of encouraging students to share ideas and these are also explained in this book. In fact, all the strategies in this book are forms of brainstorming with clearer structures. Having said this, the Brainstorm session, if used for short periods, plays a useful role in creating the correct environment for the thinking classroom.

The COMMA THINKING RULE

(No full stops, only commas)

The Comma Thinking Rule

As a teacher, I have often found it difficult to persuade students to offer more than one idea in response to a question or a stimulus situation. The result is an impoverished learning and thinking climate.

The basis for much of what happens in my classroom stems from the **Comma Thinking Rule** which is designed to be an antidote to the deadening effect of the single response.

Process

I regularly introduce learners to this rule. Firstly I draw a fairly scruffy full stop on the board, large enough for all students to see clearly. There is always a gap in the middle of the full stop to prompt greater curiosity. I ask the class, "What is this?" After the first answer, which may be "a ball", "a piece of chalk", I respond with "and...?", thus encouraging further responses, continuing to do so until a number of suggestions have been made. I encourage them to change their perception by considering 3D if none of these responses have surfaced at this point. I then ask them to view the object from the perspective of a fish with attitude swimming upside-down looking upwards or from the point of view of a bird flying through the sky and looking down at the object. Students are encouraged to be unusual and are offered positive feedback and encouragement, especially when lateral answers emerge.

Once twenty answers are offered, I draw a large comma and go through the same process. After about ten answers, I then write

Thinking Rule

and then ask the class to decode this rule. The answer for which I am looking is that Full Stops are OUT and that Commas are IN. (See graphic on left.)

You are likely to receive variations of this theme and students need to be congratulated since this demonstrates the Comma Thinking Rule. Tell students that putting a full stop after the first idea one generates, tends to limit the thinking process and that good thinkers attempt to generate as many answers or ideas as possible before settling on the best idea. Encourage them to use the Comma Thinking Rule throughout their learning. When using group-based learning, a good idea is ask each group to nominate one person as the Comma person whose job it is to remind the rest to use the Comma Thinking Rule.

Example

Look at the drawing of the stop sign (over the page) and the street lamp positioned near each other at a busy T junction. To practice the Comma Thinking Rule, I often ask students to consider which one of the objects is happier and to accompany the decision with a reason (this is of course encouraging students to analyse and evaluate). I do tell students that "Good thinkers offer a reason or reasons when they make a judgment".

Strategies such as Think:Pair:Share (p.91) or the Round Robin (p.82) can be employed here.

The Tyranny of "THE"
(Paul McCready)

What is 'the' answer?
What is 'the' way to do this?

Instead

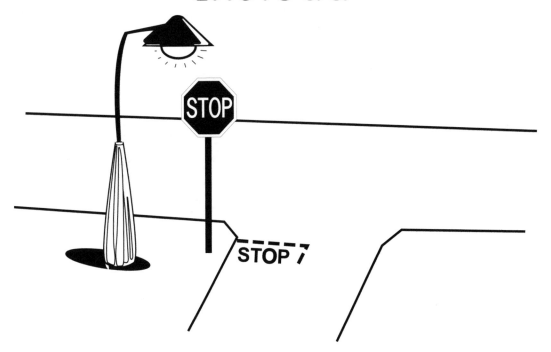

Which one is happier?
The street lamp or stop sign?

Some responses are as follows:

- the street lamp because it only works 8 hours per day
- the stop sign because it is helping people 24 hours per day
- the street lamp because it has a better view and has thousands of visitors at night (moths etc)
- the stop sign because it is low enough to make eye contact with the people in the cars and because it has the grudging gratitude of motorists
- the street lamp because it is connected to other street lamps via cabling
- the stop sign since dogs pay more attention to the larger cylindrical girth of the street lamps

and so on. This is a powerful way to encourage the use of the Comma Thinking Rule and to show the power of thinking beyond the immediate and superficial. Teachers and parents could punctuate responses by using the word 'comma' to encourage this rule. It is important not to place a value on each response as it may discourage others who wish to respond but who may feel that their answer may not be up to that standard. My standard response to brainstorming answers is 'Comma'. At the end of the session I often deal with a few of the answers in more depth and invite the class to respond to those answers.

Application

Imagine asking the following:

- Maths. Which one has more fun? + or −, x or ÷
- Language. Which one is more interesting? 'However' or 'Because'
- Chemistry. Which chemical is more influential or useful? Chemical A or B (teacher chooses)
- Design your own.

Observation

- The teacher sets and leads the classroom atmosphere. It is up to the teacher to decide whether to honour himself/herself or honour the thirty learners in terms of controlling the ideas which permeate the classroom as a result of dynamic teaching. The danger is that many teachers are dynamic in their practice but fail to realise that often that dynamism has a monopoly on expression and can overtly or covertly discourage student expression! Students soon pick up messages such as whether or not the teacher is really interested in the opinions and ideas of their students or not. The Comma Thinking Rule sends out a clear message that the teacher is interested in their ideas and is looking for six instead of one answer.

- Many apparently less able students are discouraged when teachers are looking for one or for '**the**' answer. By employing the Comma Thinking Rule, the message is clear that the teacher is looking for input rather than perfection in each question. It can be very liberating for many learners to recognise that the teacher is genuinely interested in a range of ideas and responses and is therefore interested in their ideas.

- The Comma Thinking Rule, used regularly, encourages the growth of some of the teachable characteristics of intelligent behaviours such as listening to others, considering alternatives, showing flexibility, persistence and appreciating other points of view.

- Too many people are seduced by 'the comfort of the first answer', and move onto the next question.

- I believe that in a classroom where a teacher is looking for ONE answer, the very bright and unusual thinkers say nothing. It is the convergent bright thinkers who respond. The traditionally weaker students are also disinclined to answer since they do not wish to be exposed as not knowing '**the**' answer. The 'Comma Thinking Rule' can remove this dynamic, especially when the teacher regularly uses the expression '**comma**', to encourage and elicit more responses.

P

The sustained

The most dangerous and destructive word in

Teaching and Learning

Comprehension – the Key to All Learning

Though this book deals mainly with strategies for higher order thinking, a strong statement is made here that the basis of all higher order thinking lies in the importance of understanding or comprehension in the learning process.

I and other teachers, have too often introduced a topic, given some basic facts (Knowledge) and then launched enthusiastically into the area of application, leaving some or many students floundering in bemusement and ignorance of what we are doing. Without understanding what we are learning and why we are learning something, it is unlikely, if not impossible, to go any further. We have all seen the *Huh?* expression on our students' faces and need to realise that we must consolidate the understanding level before moving on. We have even seen this amongst teachers at staff meetings when some fail to understand what is being explained or said. We also know that many adults do not wish to expose their lack of understanding and remain quietly ignorant for the remainder of that item. There is no difference in our classroom. We need to concentrate on ensuring that all our students are given the opportunity to understand what we are teaching and not assume that all have the same learning, and thus, comprehension style.

On the page *Some Strategies for Thinking at Different Levels* on page 9, which is the sheet I use to plan lessons and units of work, there is a section referring to Howard Gardner's Multiple Intelligence Model. This is one of the most significant advances in the learning process of recent times. I was privileged to listen to one of Gardner's better known advocates, Thomas Armstrong, at a conference in Sydney in January 1998. The *Using Your Brain* conference, organised by Hawker Brownlow Education, brought three inspiring educationists to Australia. They were Professor Reuven Feurersein, Jim Bellanca and Dr Thomas Armstrong, author of *Multiple Intelligences in the Classroom*.

Dr Armstrong offered a telling vignette concerning the importance of making sure people understand material presented using the power of Multiple Intelligences. He asked the one hundred or so delegates which of them understood Boyles' Law. Most of us did not. He gave us seven chances to understand.

1. Through the *Verbal-Linguistic* intelligence, he wrote on the board "For a fixed mass and temperature of gas, the pressure is inversely proportional to the volume". Most of us were no wiser.

2. He then offered the *Logical-Mathematical* explanation which was "PxV=K" or 2ATM x 4 cubic centimetres = 8 which is the same as 4ATM x 2 cubic centimetres. Understand? Most of us were still in the dark. (ATM = Atmospheres)

3. Using the *Visual-Spatial* intelligence, he asked us to imagine a painfully inflamed boil on our hand and then to imagine using the fingers of the other hand to squeeze the outer edges of the boil. More now understood the inverse proportion of what would happen to the fixed volume of liquid being squeezed. More pressure, less space with the resulting bursting of the boil.

4. The *Body-Kinesthetic* intelligence was even easier to understand. He asked to us take air into our mouth and shut our mouth so that our cheeks were slightly puffed out. Then if we were to put pressure on the left cheek, there would be less space for that volume. The volume then goes up when the pressure goes down. By this stage, all present understood.

5. For the *Musical-Rhythmic* intelligence, he introduced us to a simple rap to explain the law.

6. For the *Intrapersonal* intelligence, he asked us to shut our eyes and reflect back to a time when we were under great pressure, such as at the end of an academic year when we had few days to complete a range of tasks. Then as the days passed we could remember the pressure getting greater (fewer days left) with a larger volume of work. We then contrasted this with longer holidays with fewer things to do. So now it was easy to understand the concept of Boyles' Law that as the pressure decreased, the space expanded. One more example of scuba divers taking a large breath under high pressure many metres underwater and then ascending rapidly made it even clearer. There was the same mass of gas, but as the pressure decreased, the volume would expand with disastrous results for the diver.

The point is that spending a little more time to ensure that the class truly understands the material will result in a better learning environment and outcome. The *Multiple Intelligence Model* is therefore a significant strategy to ensure that the sustained HUH? will seldom be seen in your classroom.

The greatest compliment you can pay me as a teacher is to say

"I disagree with you for the following reasons ..."

Personal Criticism or Information?

One of the attendant features of Creating the Thinking Classroom is that of honesty of opinion.

When we invite students to criticise the information offered by other students and/or the teacher, it may be prudent to offer some ground rules.

I explain the following to students:

1. You are addressing the information/opinion/point of view, not the person.
2. There must be no attempt to belittle or disparage the person.
3. If the criticism is hurtful, don't use it. That may happen in the adult world, but does not need to be present in the classroom.
4. The only reason to criticise is to improve the quality of the thinking climate, not to damage it.
5. When someone disagrees with you, they are paying you a compliment. This is because:
   a) that person listened to you
   b) analysed your information
   c) felt it was important enough to challenge
   d) bothered to tell you.
   Therefore say "Thank you", listen to the different point of view, and either accept or reject it.

I never will forget an incident in 1976. I was making an announcement at a school assembly concerning basketball practices. I invited students to add their names to the list so that they could "partake of the sport".

As we were leaving the hall, a colleague whom I admired greatly, Linelle Irvine, said these simple words, "Eric, one partakes of food and drink – the rest is **participates**". I clearly remember saying "Thanks Linelle," because I knew the observation came with love, not destruction. I don't believe I have ever made that mistake again.

The choice is clear. We need to ensure that comments are seen and intended as information, not personal criticism. A classroom free of personal and hurtful criticism is far more likely to become a **thinking classroom**. I encourage my students to challenge the information I offer, not me. See opposite.

(P)

Bloom's Taxonomy and Learning Behaviours

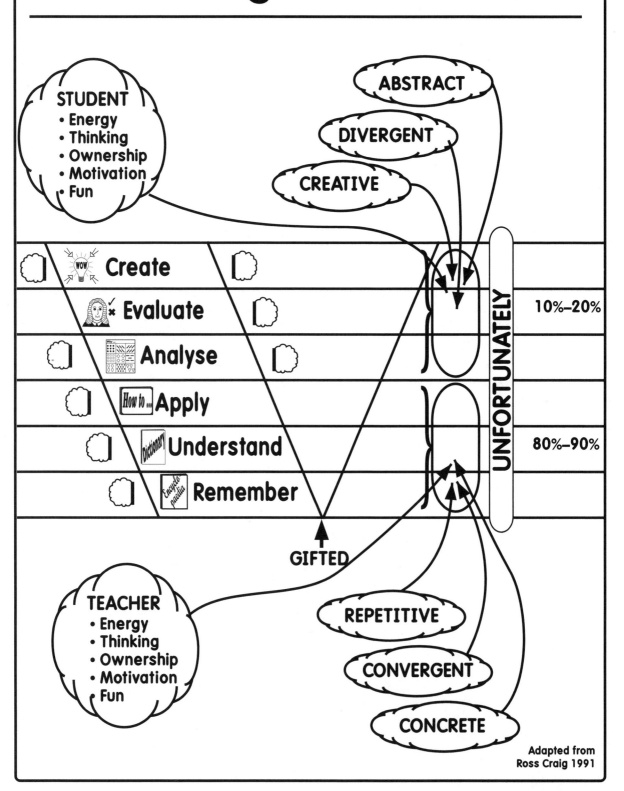

STUDENT
• Energy
• Thinking
• Ownership
• Motivation
• Fun

ABSTRACT

DIVERGENT

CREATIVE

Create

Evaluate

Analyse

Apply

Understand

Remember

UNFORTUNATELY

10%–20%

80%–90%

GIFTED

TEACHER
• Energy
• Thinking
• Ownership
• Motivation
• Fun

REPETITIVE

CONVERGENT

CONCRETE

Adapted from Ross Craig 1991

Eric Frangenheim, Rodin Educational Consultancy ©

bad? When 'Good' is Bad (Analysis and Evaluation Strategies)
good? good = bad

Often as teachers and parents, we are disappointed by the lack of any meaningful or intelligent reply from our students in response to questions such as:

"What did you think about

- the television program,
- the school camp,
- the Prime Minister's statement
- the proposal concerning ...?"

The standard response is usually '**Good**' or '**Don't know**' or something particularly negative and the discussion ends there. As teachers and parents, we are disappointed at the inability of our charges to sustain a conversation and to comment beyond the superficial – (good!) and therefore I consider '**Good**' to be '**Bad**'. As mentioned in the Introduction, it is often not the fault of our students. We simply have not offered them sufficient tools to think critically and creatively. Armed with these tools, they are usually more than able to respond with some semblance of original thought, sustain that conversation and offer proof that they are doing the thinking. When we claim that we wish to empower learners, it is by providing these tools and skills that we will help accomplish this aim.

All strategies which are offered in this book are related to my strong belief about the positive effect of Bloom's Taxonomy on Learning Behaviours. See page opposite.

In essence, I believe that when I am teaching at the lower levels of Bloom's taxonomy, I am in the 'Monkey See, Monkey Understand, Monkey Do' phase of instruction. I mean no disrespect to my colleagues but the truth is that I am supplying the information (Remember), I am doing the explaining (Understand), I am showing how it is done (Apply) and then I am asking my students to mimic me with Pavlovian obedience to prove to me that they have mastery over the material. Now there is nothing wrong with this and in fact it is a **vital** step in the learning process since if this is done well, with conviction, creativity and passion, students or learners will then be able to advance to the higher levels of thinking. However the truth is that when I am operating at those lower three levels, and I used to do this for 90% of my lessons every day, all the energy is on my side of the desk. I am doing the thinking, I am being creative in how I teach and therefore I am having the fun. Ownership and motivation in the learning process are my domain. My learners or students are only being asked to be repetitive, stick to my ways of doing things (convergent) and to operate at the concrete level most of the time since they have to operate with material which I have explained.

It is only when I move into the higher levels of Bloom's Taxonomy, when I ask them to discuss, investigate, examine (Analyse), then to select, choose, rate and prioritise (Evaluate) and finally when I challenge them to create alternatives, modify, improve (Create), that my students are thinking abstractly, creatively and divergently. It is now that energy has gone from my side of the desk to their side that they are doing the thinking, that they own the process and product, that they can draw on internal motivation and that they can have the fun. At this level, I know that I am honouring my mission statement which is '**To Promote Thinking in Learning**'.

The next few pages offer strategies that allow learners to respond at the Analyse, Evaluate and Create levels. I have offered examples from my own teaching and from those lessons I have shared with others. Once again I encourage you to use the page of SUE 1 and SUE 2 opposite each of the strategies to reflect as to how these strategies could be infused into your practice.

The chapters are:

- **PCQ (Pros, Cons, Questions)**
- **Pros:Cons:Improve**
- **SWOT Analysis**
- **The Y Chart**
- **K.W.L.**
- **Tournament Prioritising**

- **PCQ – Extension**
- **Judge Jury**
- **T Bar Analysis and Organisers**
- **The Decision Making Matrix**
- **The Silent Card Shuffle**
- **The Extent Barometer**

P. C. Q.

Topic: _____

<u>P</u>ros	<u>C</u>ons	<u>Q</u>uestions
		(• **What if…**) (• **I wonder…**) (• **It would be interesting to know…**)

Analyse and Evaluate Thinking Strategies

An Introductory Note

Though the following strategies are primarily concerned with analysis and evaluation, they are also involved with synthesis-type operations since alternatives always spring to mind. Furthermore, any form of problem solving beyond the simple and obvious requires operation in most and sometimes all six levels of Bloom's taxonomy of the cognitive domain. I often refer to the Mr Bean video where as a cinema attendant, he is preparing to meet the Queen of England at a Royal Film performance. It becomes very clear that as he frenetically attempts to rectify the several blemishes in his personal attire and hygiene, he is analysing, collecting ideas from his past but also generating some very creative solutions to his problems. Throughout the preparation, he is regularly assessing or evaluating his attempts at solving his problems. In fact, this film is Bloom's Taxonomy of the Cognitive Domain in action.

Pros, Cons and Questions

PCQ is an acronym for Pros, Cons, Questions. The term '**Pros and Cons**', has been with us almost since the beginning of time. After all, it is an attempt to offer fairness in considering proposals, ideas or suggestions. It is a wonderful antidote to the almost automatic prejudicial response that we are tempted to adopt when an idea may endanger our comfort zone. Adding the '**Questions**' dimension (see **KWL** on page 61) assists in broadening the scope of enquiry.

PCQ is a basic tool for the critical thinker, attempting to analyse any situation before deciding whether to not to support it. Drawing up a simple table (see example further down) will help the thinker to make sense of their considerations.

The '**Pros**' columns invites one to list all the benefits, strengths, plusses, advantages of the idea, from as many different points of view as possible. The second column, '**Cons**', deals with all the negatives, contra ideas, disadvantages, weaknesses of the idea and finally, the '**Questions**' column offers an opportunity for questions, probing, curiosity and 'what ifs'.

What I have found interesting is that whereas the '**Pros and Cons**' offer an opportunity for convergent and logical thinking based on the evidence or materials presented, the '**Questions**' aspect often uncovers the truly bright thinker as this is more an opportunity to display divergent pathways in thinking. Useful sentence stems to assist students in generating questions could be 'I wonder…', 'what if ….' And 'It would be interesting to know …' (see template for **PCQ** on opposite page). It is a delight to see a student getting excited when offering a truly remarkable insight under '**Questions**'. This also has the effect of encouraging others to generate 'higher order' perspectives or viewpoints and acts as a most beneficial virus in learning.

On the advice of a teacher at one of my workshops, I have added Investigate to the Interesting column. The point here is that the plus and minus of any situation or proposal is often fairly obvious, but powerful thinking is that which benefits the person and avoids future problems. Therefore, by asking intelligent questions which could be investigated, it is possible to avoid future difficulties. A personal case in point is when I was introduced to an unsavoury investment advisor a few years ago. I certainly looked at the pluses and then a few minuses, but I completely failed to heed my own beliefs in thinking in that I did not apply the Interesting. Had I asked questions such as "It would be interesting to know if the person was known to the Australian Securities Commission, if he were a long standing bankrupt, if he had been removed from his professional body, if the Tax Office were aware of him, if I could get favourable report about him from former employers and other investors", I would have avoided being burnt by him. The truth is that had I investigated any of the items under Interesting, I would have kept well away from him. I would have used head thinking instead of heart thinking, which in this case was all to do with financial progress or greed to be more honest.

An example would be to consider that the government buy every student, from Year 5 onwards, a laptop computer with a software package. Take three to six minutes to add to the **PCQ** analysis on the next page.

An important point to consider is that there must be no attempt to evaluate any of the ideas. As in any brainstorming activity, write everything down. The evaluation can take place later.

Proposal: Government to buy laptops for all Year 5-12 students		
Pros	**Cons**	**Questions**
· Increased computer sales · More employment for manufacturers and associated trades · Variety in learning process · A more computer-literate nation · Universal keyboard skilling · Teachers will be forced to learn about computers	· Taxes may have to go up · Not enough teachers trained in using computers · Students may play games instead of learning · Spread of computer bugs	· Would parents welcome it? · Would this help towards creating the *Clever Country*? · Would computers be used effectively in the curriculum? · Who would train the teachers? · Would theft decrease? · Would all students welcome this? · Would ideas on teaching improve? · Would we become known as a musical nation since so many of us would be on key?

PCQ Extension

The PCQ offered above could be deemed to be a basic analysis tool, as it offers fairness in thinking and a tool to organise the data from the stimulus material or the resources in one of three columns, P, C or Q. However, after a certain amount of time, the teacher can extend this tool (note the Icon used to denote Analyse) by consciously asking, 'How can we view the proposal from as many different perspectives as possible?' To extend the basic analysis of the proposal that the government or the education authorities buy computers for all students in Years 5-12, we could add a columns to the left for 'Perspectives', list other perspectives and complete the analysis. This is likely to result in a more rigorous 'higher order thinking'.

Proposal: Government to buy laptops for all Year 5-12 students (PCQ Extension)			
Perspectives	**Pros**	**Cons**	**Questions**
From Students point of view			
Teachers			
ICT Industry			
Parents			
Education Systems			
Future employers			

Observations

It is also possible to encourage a proactive attitude by asking students to look at the Cons list and decide how they could remove or minimise the cons before making a decision. The point is that before we make a decision, we need to analyse the situation and one way to analyse any situation or proposal is to organise the data. The PCQ thinking strategy or thinking tool is a simple yet elegant device. It needs to be encouraged as a life skill, especially for young people at risk of making disastrous decisions.

Applications

1. The PCQ tool can assist students in writing a report or assignment on a topic and offers them at least three chapters or paragraphs.

2. It can also be used as an effective self-assessment tool whereby a student examines their own work before submitting it for assessment. The Question part could be used to ask how they can improve the piece of work, especially by removing the Cons. The Pros deal with the extent to which the student has met the criteria or addressed any rubrics.

Example: *Volcanic Eruptions (Geography)*

Pros	Cons	Questions
· Increased soil fertility. · Lifeblood of many agricultural communities.	· Death and destruction. · Contribution to the greenhouse effect.	· Where are the top ten killer-volcanoes?

'Pros : Cons : Improve' and Story Writing

In terms of drafting and editing and critical literacy, this strategy is extremely efficient. The example below has been developed for Grades 2–5 but can be adapted to any grade. Use this as a lesson plan should you be caught short one day!

Process

STEP 1   Build up expectation that the students are about to witness a great short story being written

STEP 2   Show them your 'fantastic' story by writing this on the board and triumphantly turning around on completion and asking the students what they think of 'it'.

A Brilliant Short Story

Yestiday I whent to the shoppe and then I bort a pie and then a newspapir and then I whent home and I ait the pie and the newspaper and I thourt that that was another grate day

STEP 3   Class Pros:Cons:Improve (Smiley Face, Sad Face and Question Mark Face)

After a few hoped for comments such as 'fantastic', (I live in hope!) I ask them to reflect by using the Pros:Cons:Improve chart. For the 'Pros' column (smiley face), I have received comments such as 'it's short' and sometimes even 'good' (my pet hate word! See p 41).

At the 'Cons' (sad face) column I am usually deluged with a chorus of negative criticism. There are trivial complaints concerning spelling (we list or number these), the confusion about what I 'ait', the fact that it was not interesting (some ungrateful wretches even suggesting quite brazenly that it might even be boring!). Others complain there are too few people, too little action, it is too short and that there is an absence of adverbs and adjectives. Of course, many notice the fact that there is a surfeit of 'and thens'.

After regaining my composure, I draw a third column with the word 'Improve' at the head. I often draw a question mark-type face as well and ask the students how I should fix or improve the story. Apart from spelling, I receive suggested adjectives and adverbs, and am encouraged to populate my story with old ladies on scooters, dog and car chases and the obligatory robber pursued by yours truly or the law.

STEP 4   I then rewrite the story using ideas from Pros:Cons:Improve. I ask the students if that is better. They agree. They soon get the message that they are indeed to be thanked, since the story came from their Pros:Cons:Improve.

STEP 5   Students submit 30-40 word story. The topic could be 'The beach, a seagull and an ice-cream' OR 'The supermarket, a rat and a pyramid of baked bean tins'.

STEP 6   I select one of these stories to write on the white board I simply make up a story, letting the **students believe it belongs to one of them.**

STEP 7   The class then completes another three-column Pros:Cons:Improve, showing concentration on the 'Cons' part.

STEP 8   Students now use the ideas on the Pros:Cons:Improve to rewrite their story so that it is 'even better'. (See page 120)

Observations

Students really do enjoy this lesson since they experience success and a sense of ownership over the process. I also believe that this is a genuine attempt at critical literacy and is a part of higher order thinking.

Applications

I have used the same process with a Grade 12 design in technology class, displaying a poor logo. This could also be used with diets, itineraries, budgets, demonstrations in Science or sport, designs for furniture or buildings, newspaper reports and definitions.

Judge Jury

Gerard Alford

This is a cooperative learning strategy that involves students arguing a case on a debatable issue in the setting of a court. It requires two students to *analyse the issue* from opposite perspectives and then prepare and present their opposing cases. A third student listens and *evaluates* both viewpoints and delivers his/her verdict.

Process

Step 1. **The Topic**: A debatable issue is chosen by the teacher, such as 'drugs in sport are inevitable, so should be allowed'.

Step 2. **The Roles**: Assign a number to each student, being 1, 2 or 3. If there is a shortage of numbers, the teacher could either fill in the numbers, or assign the remaining students as number 3s.
- The number 1s present a 90 second argument FOR the topic (The Defence)
- The number 2s present a 90 second argument AGAINST the topic (The Prosecution)
- The number 3s decide the outcome of the case and present their verdict. (The Judge & Jury)

Step 3. **Research & Planning**

 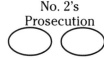 

a. The students individually research/prepare their case.
b. The number 1's ('defence counsellors') meet in groups of 3–5 to prepare their case
c. The number 2's ('the prosecution') meet separately in groups of 3– 5 to prepare their case.
d. The 'Judges' meet to discuss the main points of the case, to anticipate the points of the defence and the prosecution and to develop criteria for deciding the case.

Step 4. **The Court Hearing**

a. The number 1's are allowed 90 seconds to present the defence's case to the Judge. After allowing time for the judges to make some notes, a 90 second argument is presented by the prosecution. Note: To foster a courtroom atmosphere, ask both parties to refer to the Judge as 'Your Honour'.
b. Again, after allowing time for the judges to make some notes, the number 1's are allowed a 30 second right of reply.
c. The Judges are allowed 1 minute to complete their judgement and then present their findings one by one to the class. The judges may begin their address with "After considering the views of the defence and the prosecution, I find in favour of ....".

   The judges must then justify their decision by evaluating the arguments of the defence and the prosecution
d. A master of the arguments for and against may be recorded on the whiteboard during the judgements for students to record in their notebooks

Observation

Students tend to respond well to the courtroom context and being allowed the time to prepare their speech in a group before delivering their speech individually, which some could otherwise find quite threatening. This strategy tends to generate a lot of energy as there is a lot of movement and activity occurring. Therefore, it is a great afternoon activity.

Applications

Secondary: Science – recycling is very inefficient and should not be supported.
Religious Education – the three monotheistic religions should be taught in all schools.
English – which social group is most marginalised in this text?

Senior Primary: Litter – creating litter should be a goal offence.

Middle Primary: Holidays – there should be twice as many holidays.

Junior Primary: Television – children should be allowed to watch as much television as they want.

SWOT Analysis

This is an extremely useful strategy for examining one's practice or organisation, such as one's club, family, school department, school, P & C or important proposals, decisions or suggestions. There are many applications in curriculum as well. This commonly used method involves categorising both internal and external factors as **Strengths**, **Weaknesses**, **Opportunities** and **Threats** (SWOT). Generally, though not exclusively, the **strengths** and **weaknesses** are internal factors relating to the organisation itself, while **opportunities** and **threats** arise externally. In non-organisational situations such as proposals, the internal-external factors are not always clearly divided.

Process

1. Decide carefully on the topic to be discussed or analysed
2. Create a SWOT template as on the opposite page
3. Write the issue to be discussed next to the heading *Topic*:
4. Complete the operation

Example

If the topic is 'My Classroom Practice':

Strengths would include factors such as your knowledge and enthusiasm level, relationship with your students, ability to motivate and inspire, lesson preparation and many other obvious aspects of your practice. However, one may also include ideas such as the quality of your own friends (could they address your classes occasionally?), jokes, anecdotes, musical ability, your travels, slides, photographs, music collection, sense of humour. How about your comfort level with more recent education theories, learning styles, behaviour management techniques and other issues affecting classrooms today? In short, any resources and capacities which allow you to undertake your professional practice and to fulfil its purpose and needs. You need to be honest in listing those areas where others consider you to be particularly strong.

Weaknesses will require a high level of honesty and self-analysis. I am aware that at certain schools, teachers invite their students to conduct a similar exercise on their teaching practice. Now that is brave behaviour! However, since I also like to keep in mind the saying, "If you always do what you always did, you'll always get what you always got!", especially if things are not going too well, being honest about one's weaknesses is the best place to start any remediation. In addition, one should also look at limitations, barriers and defects in the overall operation which prevent or hinder one from fulfilling one's potential. These may be mentioned in the Threats quadrant since these are external.

Opportunities are normally to be found outside one's immediate operation. If one of the weaknesses is discomfort at addressing larger groups of people, then joining an organisation such as Toastmasters is an **opportunity** to overcome that weakness. Often the help or solution is to be found within the school or within one's immediate community.

Threats are often more difficult to determine or imagine. Teachers are becoming increasingly aware of the threats of stress, keeping up to date, satisfying paper-work demands and a raft of considerations extraneous to classroom practice. One way of meeting or eliminating some of these threats is to utilise one's strengths, e.g., if you are good at goal setting. Another threat for many teachers and parents is the march of technology and the need to be *au fait* with these developments. One way of meeting these threats is then to avail oneself of workshops offering training in these areas.

Observation

When analysing a situation or proposal (e.g., my classroom practice, the school sports carnival, the effectiveness of our family, the introduction of a Goods and Services Tax, Hitler's decision to invade Russia in 1941, etc) the ensuing open brainstorm usually results in a dog's breakfast of ideas. Consequently, it is difficult to organise the various ideas and therefore almost impossible to arrive at a useful resolution or decision.

S.W.O.T. Analysis

Topic:

Strengths ·

Weaknesses ·

Opportunities · · · · · · · · · · · · · · · · · ·

Threats ·

Action 1

Action 2

Eric Frangenheim, Rodin Educational Consultancy

Ⓟ

Using a **SWOT** Analysis allows thinkers to view the results of their deliberations in a more ordered and manageable manner (Analysis), decide on a solution or alternative (Synthesis) and if there is more than one possible action, to decide on the best action (Evaluation) and to monitor that action for appropriateness and success (Evaluation). For this reason, I have added *Action 1* and *Action 2* to the template so that one is able to move beyond the Analysis function.

Applications

1. Apart from the applications used above within a general classroom lesson plan, another important application lies in the area of personal assignments or projects. As a teacher, I have seen too many distressed students who have come to the realisation four weeks into their assignment that it is not going anywhere simply because it does not suit them or there simply was insufficient research material. Expecting students to apply a **SWOT** Analysis on their proposed project would avoid expending energy unprofitably in the future, especially if one of the items under Weakness is a dearth of material on the topic to be researched.

2. Many students, once they have chosen a topic, lack the ability of knowing where and how to start. The **SWOT** Analysis format provides a structure in itself for the assignment. Consider a student who wishes to tackle a topic such as the GST. By following the **SWOT** structure, the student would have sufficient well-organised material to answer the question whether or not the proposal is suitable or not. Each quadrant could be a chapter or paragraph of the main body of the assignment.

3. Teachers are often faced with important decisions such as changing styles of teaching, taking on further study, moving interstate, setting their sights on promotion or even changing careers. The use of a **SWOT** Analysis or the **PCQ** will more likely ensure a more considered decision.

A Note on Analytical and Critical Thinking Environments

Terri and I always encouraged our three girls to say 'thank you' when a teacher corrected them in class since the teacher is motivated to help their students grow and make them 'even better'.

More recently I have read some of Stephen Covey's work in 'Seven Habits of Effective Families'. In Habit 1, he makes a point about criticism which could have great currency in the classroom. He contends that after stimulus, e.g., as in some negative comment, we have a choice to pause before we respond. Normally we respond in anger or disappointment. He suggests we could pause to choose whether to see the comment as **personal criticism** or as **useful information**. This is why his comments resonate so strongly with us.

It is sometimes difficult to encourage people to be honest as in the W of SWOT, especially if you ask colleagues to conduct a SWOT Analysis of your teaching, your department of school. As a result, we need to clearly explain that we intend to regard anything in the W section as '**information**' and not as '**personal criticism**'.

A Note on Analytical and Critical Thinking Environments

Stimulus ————————————▶ Response

e.g. a comment made in **W of SWOT**   anger, disappointment, closed mind

Choice to Pause
Is the comment • Personal Criticism?
or • Information?

Excerpted from *The 7 Habits of Highly Effective Families* by Stephen R. Covey © 1999 S Covey.
Reprinted with permission from Franklin Covey Co., www.franklincovey.com. All rights reserved.

SUE 1 _____

SUE 2 _____

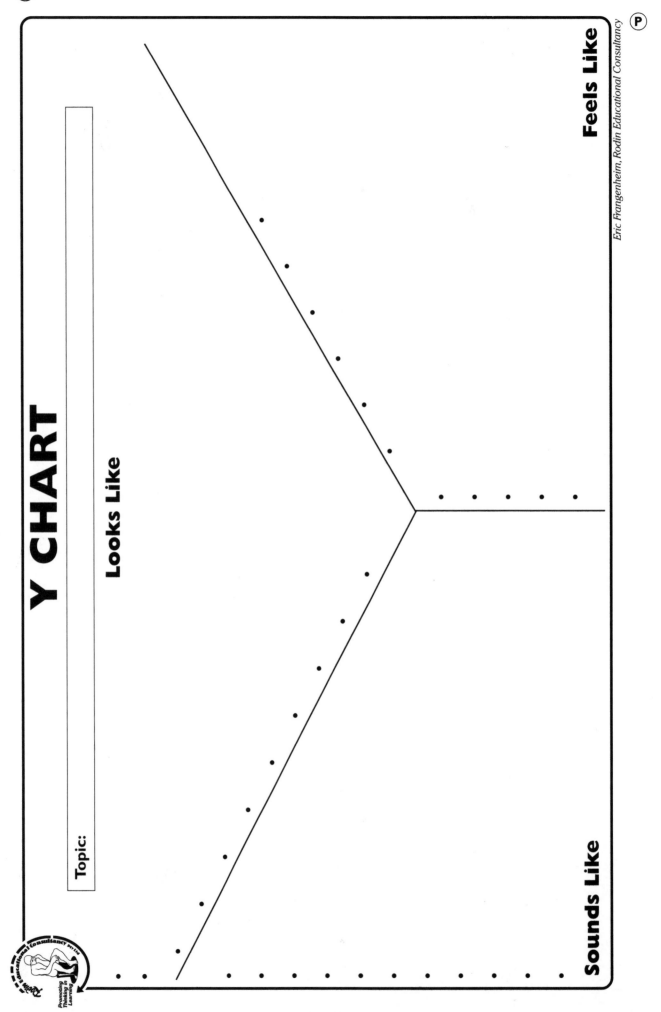

Y CHART

Topic:

Looks Like

Sounds Like

Feels Like

Y Chart Analysis

This is an effective strategy enabling learners to respond to a situation, proposal, problem, stimulus material or most situations which demand some thinking, some discussion, response or analysis. It relies far more on the senses, intuition and imagination than is the case with the **SWOT Analysis** or **PCQ**. Though I use the term loosely, the **Y Chart** is more of a right brain analysis than the more 'left brained' **PCQ** and **SWOT** Analysis.

Process

1. Decide on the topic to be discussed and analysed; e.g., 'Leadership'. This was the topic in a Year 6 all-day unit on Sir Charles Franklin, the explorer who died attempting to find a North-West sea passage through Canada. The students were asked to write an advertisement for a leader of this expedition with the selection criteria necessary.

2. Draw up a simple Y Chart (see opposite) with the topic filled out, in this case Leadership Qualities.

3. In the 'Looks Like' segment, brainstorm all that you would see a good leader doing, everything you would expect to see happening around a good and effective leader, what the leader may look like and most importantly everything you think you would be able to see behind the scenes which would have contributed to the final product. By this I encourage students to employ what I call their X Ray eyes. For example, did the leader have a childhood full of personal challenges such as in sport, adventure, overcoming personal difficulties, involvement in community service and projects and even application at school.

4. In the 'Sounds Like' segment, brainstorm all the sounds associated with an effective leader, such as clear commands, clarification of task, delegation and encouragement. Include the types of words one would expect a leader to use on the people she/he is leading and the sort of words or phrases members of the team are likely to say to each other about the leader and to the leader. Once again, with X Ray hearing, what could one imagine a leader would be thinking or saying to him/herself and the sort of conversations or sounds associated with her/his past, e.g., the sounds of a referees whistle or applause or the use of the word 'We' instead of 'Me'.

5. In the 'Feels Like' segment, brainstorm all that you would expect to feel in a tactile/kinesthetic sense as well as in an emotional response to the quality of leadership. Feels like may include a sense of team-work, corporate or group direction, commitment, success, pride, achievement, challenge, etc.

6. From the information above, there should be sufficient raw material to design an advertisement with related selection criteria for the required team leader. This was done extremely successfully in the Year 6 class.

Observation

- Not only has the student completed a form of analysis on the topic of leadership, the student can now synthesise the raw material into an advertisement. In this case, both critical and creative thinking has been employed. The word "Good" has been avoided and the student has engaged in meaningful thinking drawing on his/her own experiences as well as observation and general knowledge.

- The **Y Chart** can be completed individually by each student or can be used in conjunction with a **Round Robin** (Noisy or Quiet) or with a **Hot Potato** (Noisy or Quiet) where one segment at a time is developed.

Possible Applications

1. This is a wonderful strategy for students who are sitting for the Writing Task in the Core Skills Test in Year 12 in Queensland. Students are offered a double sheet of stimulus material in the form of visuals or text. Many students are overwhelmed by the choice on offer and may take some time to get started. My advice is that they select either one or two areas of the stimulus material. If it is to be a single item, the student applies the Y Chart Analysis as in the Leadership example. Recently there was a picture of a pair of farmer's boots used as a visual stimulus for country life. Applying the Y Chart, a group of 80 Year 12 students spent 90 seconds on each segment. Nearly all of them generated ten ideas in each segment of the Y Chart, offering them thirty ideas with which to put together a written response on country life. In the 'Looks Like' segment, ideas such as a challenge, lonely, tyranny of distance, letters from banks, relatives, boarding school children, climate, highs and lows, a variety of farm animals and machinery, a large range of visuals associated with farming and the developments likely to eventuate. The 'Sounds Like' segment produced ideas such as rain, thunder, lightning, tractors and harvesters, the sounds of animals, sounds of elation, frustration, despair, comments such as "we'll fight on", "we'll manage", "we've done it!", conversations with neighbours and family over the telephone etc. The 'Feels Like' segment raised ideas on loneliness, success, elation, frustration, unity, fear, optimism, hope, feelings of grit, sweat, satisfaction, the taste of good food, rain on the face and so on.

2. When working with a group of Heads of Department who were involved in a process to revitalise their individual departments, I made the suggestion that they could complete two Y Charts. The topic for the first analysis could be 'My Department Today', and for the second the topic could be 'My Department – the Ideal'. Having done this, they could then invite the members of the department to complete the same exercise (see my note on Criticism and Information on page 35) using the headings, 'Our Department Today' and 'The Ideal'.

3. When acting as facilitator for a strategic planning and goal-setting session at a school, the members present (including teachers, Board members, cleaners, grounds staff, kitchen and boarding staff), we completed a similar exercise to the one above. The two topics were a) the school today and b) the school beyond AD2000. (See my note on Criticism and Information on page 35).

4. A suggestion I make in my workshops with parents is to look at the quality of their family. Keeping in mind my misgivings about the statement "If it ain't broke, don't fix it" (it may not be broke but could it be better?), I offer the suggestion that one way of improving family life is to do a two part Y Chart. The first Y Chart would consider 'Our Family Now' and the second would consider 'Our Family – The Ideal'. (See my note on Criticism and Information on page 35).

5. Creative writing – if asking students to write on a topic, e.g., A Nutty Professor, applying the Y Chart will lead to strong imagery in the 'Looks Like' segment. 'Sounds Like' will reveal comments of associates such as "Oh no!" 'Feels Like' will deal with frustration and embarrassment, etc.

6. In guidance situations, such as those dealing with bullying, asking the bully to complete the Y Chart can be a powerful learning experience especially when the facilitator asks the bully to imagine what the victim's home would 'Look Like, Sound Like, Feel Like'. This could include sad parents, poor reports, reluctance to go to school, feelings of low self-worth, etc. Change usually comes from within once self-awareness is present!

Examples of Y Charts from students at various schools follow on page 49. You will notice both concrete and abstract ideas and some very insightful thinking.

The Dirty Dancing Y Chart was based on a 12 minute section of the film where the teacher is leading a new student. The Swimming Pool Y Chart used the video/DVD from the excellent 'Discovering Democracy' kit showing Charles Perkins highlighting the local council laws regarding the use of public swimming pools in the 1960s.

SUE 1

SUE 2

Some examples of Y Charts

1. Dirty Dancing – Year 12 English, Bourke High School, Hazel Patow

Looks Like	Sounds Like	Feels Like
· Teacher and student · Revealing desires · Change · Communication · Hesitancy (non verbal) · Fear of failure · Performance · Fear of success · Audience – audience · Trust of learner to judgement teacher and then · Possibility of negative teacher to learner or positive reaction · A belief that he/she · Pressure of fear can teach anyone · Testing of weaknesses · Closer friendship and strength · Love · Courage · Evolution · Risk-taking · Clothing then less clothing	· Demanding teacher · Defensive · Assertive · Challenge to authority · "I've got a lot to learn" · "I can do it!" · "She's hopeless!" · "This can work" · Boos and applause · "Don't mess this up!" · Going through the rules and steps before the competition · Encouraging each other	· Frustration · Newness · Different world · New culture · Exploration · Awkward · Attraction · Danger · Inadequacy · Rebellion · Self-doubt · Fear · Loss of father's trust · Betrayal

2. Gallipoli – Year 9 English., Ipswich State High School, Helen Rivers
Stimulus – Last 8 minutes of film

Looks Like		Sounds Like	Feels Like	
· Trenches · Misery · Friends dying · No happy faces · Dead bodies · Insane · Bayonets · Fear · Blood · Dust · Diseases · Dirt · Death · Turks · Machine guns · Kill others · Tears · Kill or be killed		· Gun Shots · Cries for help · "Please don't blow the whistle" · Prayers · Sombre · Voices of family · Silence · Wind through the flags	· Racing heart · Depressed · Suicide · Insane · Fear · Futile · Scared · Useless · Patriotic · Senseless · Brave · No purpose · Sense of stupidity · No point · Anxiety	
Pathos – feeling Sympathy – feeling 'for' Antipathy – feeling 'against' Apathy – 'nil' feeling Empathy – feeling 'as if'			Last 8 minutes of file "Gallipoli" Year 9 class • mostly lower interest level • activity created heightened engagement	

3. Swimming Pool Protests (Charles Perkins) – Year 7, Harristown State School, Maureen Meehan and Maree Nolan

Looks Like		Sounds Like	Feels Like	
· Sadness – sad faces · Power · Frustration · Angry · Unfairness community · Anger · Absence of · Helplessness freedom · Racism · Controlling · Discrimination · Protest · Kids being washed · People · Confusion swimming · Status quo · Banners · Embarrassment · The bus · Neglect · Charles Perkins · Difference in jobs · Racist pool · Angry parents · Rough houses · Jealousy · Upset children · Prejudice		· Shouting · Abusive language · Racist comments · Hatred · Put downs · "Are we doing the right thing?" · "Why can't we be treated the same?" · Annoyance · Sad voices · The bell · Freedom · Caged freedom · Arguing the point · Protest songs · Verbal abuse	· Anger · Shame · Pain · Hopelessness · Sadness · Confusion · Hatred · Powerlessness · Jealousy · Hurt · Fear · Helplessness · Not belonging · Disgust · Abandonment · Depression · Blame · Failure · Self pity · Like dirt · Sick · Embarrassment · Disappointment · Revenge · Frustration · Pushed around · Neglect · Self-hatred · Annoyance	

3 : 2 : I RIQ

Gerard Alford

Since senior students can only effectively process one-way lecture style information for 12-15 minutes, time should be regularly set aside for students to process and make sense of the new information. The 3:2:1 RIQ strategy is a structure that assists students to process new information. Though it starts simply at the data retrieval level (Recall), the next two stages will clearly lead to **Higher Order Thinking** and reveal depths of **insight** and **questioning**.

Process

Step 1   After the reading of a novel, a poem or a short story, or after watching a video or as a review of course work or a field trip, a 3:2:1 RIQ is completed **individually** by students.

> **3 Recalls:**   Students state **3 facts** they can recall from the course work completed to date, an article, a report, a short story or video they have just read or watched.

> **2 Insights:**   This can be such things as why the material is relevant, who it affects, the implications, how it relates to themselves/society/school, and identifying correlations, connections and patterns.

> **1 Question**   These may include:
> - I do not understand why ....?
> - How does this affect ....?
> - In the future, what will ....?
> - What is the relevance of ....?
> - How does this relate to ....?

Step 2:   **The Interview**

Students are allocated a partner and take turns at stating their 3:2:1 RIQ. Encourage the student listening to ask questions such as:
- Do you mean ....?
- Are you saying that ......?
- What do you mean by ....?

Also, encourage students to discuss and perhaps even answer the questions posed by their partner.

By allowing students the opportunity to articulate their thoughts in the 3:2:1 RIQ structure, deep conversation is occurring and an opportunity is given for students to express any misunderstandings in a non-threatening situation. It also gives some students the opportunity to act as the teacher!

Step 3:   **Class Recall**

The teacher may ask for some of the more interesting recalls, insights and questions as a class. This can be effective feedback for the teacher to ensure that students have recalled the main concepts as well as to ascertain whether some concepts require revisiting in order to facilitate better student understanding.

Observation

We all know there is very little point progressing with course work if there are a number of students who do not understand the work covered to date. In this context, the 3:2:1 RIQ can act as a **safety-valve** for both students and the teacher to ascertain the class's understanding, and therefore could be employed at regular intervals, such as every week or fortnight.

Applications

Analysing Companies (Business)

3 Recalls: The PE Ratio, the Company's activities and the current share price.

2 Insights: The trend of the company share price in relation to its competitors.

The outlook of the industry.

1 Question: Can the company increase its market share?

Deconstructing a Press Release (English)

3 Recalls: Names, positions and location.

2 Insights: The company wants this released as widely as possible.

The company wants to appear as favourable as possible.

1 Question: Whose story are we not given?

The Silent Card Shuffle

Eric Frangenheim

I first started using this strategy in the primary school lesson on The Reconciliation of Goldilocks and the Three Bears. This is one of my whole-day lessons which I use for the Grades 3–5 students with the purpose of demonstrating the infusion of thinking strategies into the regular curriculum. I often use this exercise with high school teachers and parents.

It is a different way of reminding students of the sequence of events and has other applications.

Process

1. Decide on the material to be sequenced and transfer the images or words onto separate cards. For example, I have 14 pictures of the story of Goldilocks and The Three Bears taken from my book "*The Reconciliation of Goldilocks and the Three Bears*".

2. To increase the amount of thinking, take two of these cards and duplicate them, so that there are 16 cards (an example of eight cards is opposite).

3. Organise your students into groups of three or four and place one envelope containing the 16 cards on each table, telling them that after you have explained the rules, they are to arrange the cards in the correct sequence so that their display tells the story. Duplicates may not be side by side and must be used.

4. Write the four step rules on the board and explain them. The four steps are
   - **Silent Card Shuffle**
   - **Justify and Refine**
   - **Circulate and Observe**
   - **Return and Refine**

Rules

Step 1 Open the envelope, spread the cards out on the table, and without any talking or whispering, rearrange the cards in to two horizontal rows of eight cards. (**Silent Card Shuffle**)

Step 2 Once the cards have been sequentially arranged, members of the group may talk and question each other about the moves, asking them to justify their decisions. They may make changes to the sequence as a result of this discussion. (**Justify and Refine**)

Step 3 The teacher now needs to orchestrate the movement of the groups so that they can visit other tables to discuss and observe the sequencing of other groups. As they move around, they are to discuss what they notice and decide if the various sequencing makes sense or not. (**Circulate and Observe**) They must not touch the cards.

Step 4 Each group returns to their home base and decides whether to refine their sequence as a result of what they have observed. (**Return and Refine**)

If they feel that no changes are necessary, they may look slightly smug!

🤔 SUE 1 _____	🤔 SUE 2 _____
_____	_____
_____	_____
_____	_____
_____	_____

PROPERTIES OF QUADRILATERALS

Trapezium	Parallelogram	Rectangle	Rhombus	Square	Kite
Only 1 pair of parallel sides	Opposite sides are parallel	Opposite sides are parallel	Opposite sides are parallel	Opposite sides are parallel	No sides are usually parallel
Diagonals may not be equal	Opposite sides are equal	Opposite sides are equal	All sides are equal	All sides are equal	Two pairs of adjacent sides are equal
	Opposite angles are equal	All angles equal 90°	Opposite angles are equal	All angles equal 90°	One pair of opposite angles are equal
	Diagonals may not be equal	Diagonals are equal	Diagonals may not be equal	Diagonals are equal	Diagonals cross each other at right angles with one diagonal being bisected
	Diagonals bisect each other	Diagonals bisect each other	Diagonals bisect each other at right angles	Diagonals bisect each other at right angles	Is also is a square
		Is also a parallelogram	Opposite sides are parallel	Is also a parallelogram	Is also is a rhombus
			Is also a parallelogram	Is also a rectangle	
			Is also a kite	Is also a rhombus	
				Is also a kite	

What is challenging about this Silent Card Shuffle is that each quadrilateral has a different number of attributes, leading to some intense thinking and explanation. (Steve Barnett, Kotara High School, NSW)

Debriefing

After I have made any final debriefing comments as to the sequencing, and the cards have been packed away, I apply a second level of debriefing by which I hope to encourage certain values in learning and group work. I ask the students to relax, close their eyes and answer the following questions silently in their heads. Some of the questions could be:

- What did you find was the most frustrating part about the whole process?

- What was the easiest part?

- What was the most difficult part?

- What did you do to encourage other members of your team to be part of the thinking?

- In which ways did you compliment other members of your team?

- What would you do differently next time so that you could improve team-work?

- What did you do particularly well?

- And finally I ask "What was the most important thing you noticed about learning?" and I open this to whole class feed-back. Tolerating ambiguity and differences is a usual response.

Note:

1. Steps 3 & 4 are optional if you are pressed for time. This means you can go straight to the teacher debriefing after Step 2 if necessary.

2. I have seen various forms of debriefing. The obvious one would be to display the "answer" on the board or OHP. However, I have seen many teachers employ more creative and effective debriefings by using question and answer type interaction. Many use this situation to praise their students for the way in which they have justified their answers or constructed meaning.

3. Do not think that one has to have wonderful drawings for a successful Silent Card Shuffle. Most of the ones in which I am involved are simply hand written and hand drawn, using a 3 x 8 folded A4 piece of paper. When becoming more sophisticated, we use a word processor and tables. To keep the Multiple Intelligences in mind, we often use text, simple pictures or icons, symbols, numbers, fractions, moods and metaphors mixed in the one Silent Card Shuffle. It is a better idea to use cardboard rather than plain paper since it is less likely to blow away

4. This strategy employs most of the Multiple Intelligence Model. Most students appreciate the silent part since it forces them to do their own thinking and construct their own meanings and understandings.

Applications:

- Sequencing as in Goldilocks, or as in the digestive system – use simple word cards.

- Classification. At Stanthorpe State School in 1998, we had 92 cards to be classified into six groups such as insects, mammals, birds, etc. The Grade 3 class coped admirably and Jo Vetter, their teacher, was visibly proud of their flexible thinking (we had included the word fly on three cards with the rule that the same word could not appear twice in the same classification). I clearly remember her comment that another plus for this activity was that she could diagnose problems at a glance.

- Matching concepts and definitions. A simple rule is if you have ten concepts, then have thirteen definitions otherwise the last few matches could be too easy. Some teachers use pictures as a third set of cards to broaden the range of intelligences being used

- Mapping and positioning is when a map, a drawing (the heart, the human body) or template (Invoice, formal letter, circuit board) is used as the base on which a range of cards has to be positioned.

- Creative Writing – see p.55. Draw the cards yourself and follow the process.

Reconciliation of Goldilocks and the Three Bears

—

Pirate Cards

(Artwork by Mick Powell, Gold Coast, Qld.)

All of a sudden	**because**	the treasure ship sailed	At last it was time
to my surprise	**However**	in spite of this	When we arrived there
Later	when the ship sank	After he walked the plank	**Luckily**
the pirate hunter appeared	**before**	Then I heard	**therefore**

Card Shuffle and Writing

Eric Frangenheim

Process

Step 1: Teams of 2. Open envelope and lay out cards.

Step 2: Teacher nominates criteria.

    e.g.: Orientation — 3 picture cards
          Complication — 6 picture cards and 2 cohesive ties
          Resolution — 3 picture cards and 1 cohesive tie

Step 3: Pairs complete a story. Encourage them to use their own words as well.

Step 4: Pair A visits Pair B. Pair B tells story. Pair A makes 2 recommendations.

Step 5: Pair B visits Pair A — same as above.
Then improve story using recommendations.
Pair A visits Pair C. Pair B visits Pair D, etc.

Step 6: Teacher nominates 2–4 pairs to display to class.

Step 7: Read and discuss.
Use 5 Ws and 1 H (Who, Where, What, When, Why and How).
Debrief.

What Happened to the Romanov Family?

Source 6: The Execution Room

Step 1   What does "to what extent" mean? *Strategy 1:3:Share*

Step 2   Look at the 'Extent Barometer'. Explain it. *Strategy 1:3:Share*

Step 3   Complete the 'Extent Barometer'.

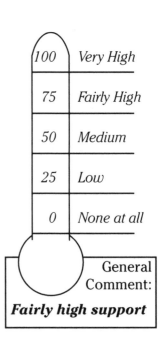

Source 5: Sir Charles said	Source 6 Extent
There were holes in the wall and floor	*Very high*
The victims were shot when kneeling	*Medium/ fairly high*
It is supposed that five were shot here	*High*
The soldiers were in a fit of rage and panic when they shot the Romanovs	*Low to none at all*

100	*Very High*
75	*Fairly High*
50	*Medium*
25	*Low*
0	*None at all*

General Comment:
Fairly high support

Extent Barometer
Eric Frangenheim

I believe that many students under-perform in examinations, not so much because they do not know the material, but simply because they often do not understand the question. (Refer to the *Empowered Learners* wall chart on page 6.)

I have found this particularly true of "To what extent..." type questions, such as "To what extent did (chemical or person's name) affect the outcome of (process or event)" or, "To what extent was (person's name) responsible for the outbreak of (event)". This is clearly an **Analysis** and ultimately an **Evaluation** question, yet many students fail to understand this and succumb to the standby of telling the story (Knowledge & Comprehension) and as a result, fail or under-perform.

This is a major reason that I believe it is important for teachers to use the Language of Bloom's Taxonomy (see Bloom Wall Chart p120) since empowered learners are those who:

a) understand the level of the question (Bloom)

b) understand the Expected Outcome, e.g., a decision (Evaluation) and

c) employ an appropriate strategy, e.g., **Extent Barometer**.

To illustrate the use of the strategy, the learning context is taken from the Extension Unit, 'What Happened to the Romanov Family?' where students are asked:

> *"To what extent does the photograph of the execution room (Source 6) support Sir Charles Elliott's report?" (Source 5)*

On the opposite page I have reprinted parts of the Student Response Booklet, which show the three-step process I use employing the 1:3:Share Strategy. I have filled in the answers which most students offer, and have annotated these for explanation.

1. There is clear evidence that there were holes in the wall and floor, therefore Very High Extent.

2. Most holes are in the lower part of the wall, but since there are a few holes higher up, we cannot say Very High or complete, but rather Fairly High or Medium.

3. By comparing the width of a person with that of a normal door, it is clear that five (5) people could have been lined up from the left up to the door, and shot there. Furthermore, students also have a floor plan in the classroom based on a plan with measurements in their booklet, so they are able to work it out 'in situ'. Note: we are not saying that five (5) **were** shot there, simply that five **could** have been shot there. Therefore Very High extent.

4. Initial arguments point to the high shots suggesting the shooters/executioners were in a state of rage and panic especially since it is stated by Elliott that the victims had been shot when kneeling. Since the execution was done at almost point blank range (11 victims and 12 soldiers in a room 5.5 metres wide by 3.5 metres deep), this view is quite understandable. However, calmer students soon ask the question "If that were true, how come there were no holes in the door?" This then leads to the conclusion that there is no support for this particular claim.

Therefore the Overall Support of the photograph for the report is Medium to Fairly High, based on 2 x Very High, 1 x Fairly High and 1 x None.

Observation

- This is clearly decision making based on an analysis of the report and the photograph. Not all students agree with each other but I feel that is part of the value of thinking. The energy is with the students, not the teacher.
- This type of question can lead to a high degree of debate amongst students.
- Students are exposed to a situation whereby they realise how important it is to analyse before they can evaluate.
- This is a useful opportunity to offer reflection on unfair behaviour. I often ask students if they have ever been hurt by unfair comments by their peers, especially when they know that there is only a small grain of truth in what has been said about them. The truth is that a judgment (Evaluation) has been made without facts (Knowledge) and a fair consideration (Analysis) being brought to bear. The moral is clear – do not judge without having the facts and organising those facts.

T Bar Analysis and Organiser (Analysis)

This is a simple and quick strategy to extract information from a text of any form of stimulus material, and present it visually on the board or in exercise books.

A	B
· _____	· _____
· _____	· _____
· _____	· _____
· _____	· _____

It is used for comparing two (2) sources or stimuli. What can seem a simple comprehension exercise in fact becomes higher order thinking, especially if a second question "Can you explain why there are such differences between the sources?"

I have included an example from the Romanovs Extension unit concerning the execution of the Russian royal family by the Bolsheviks in 1918. Judge Sergeyev's findings (he was the first Chief investigator) are reported by Judge Sokolov, his successor, in Source 3 and by an American Reporter in Source 4. Both Judge Sergeyev and Judge Sokolov were part of the White Government, opposed to the Reds (Communists). The investigation took place after the Reds had vacated the town in which the execution took place.

Step 1   What are all the differences between these two accounts of what Judge Sergeyev is supposed to have said? (See p.59.)

Source 3 – JUDGE SOKOLOV	*Source 4 – AMERICAN REPORTER*
• Entire family was executed	• Only five (5) were executed
• Reported 1 February 1919	• Reported December 1918
• Russian	• American
• Judge	• Reporter
• Definite language – "no doubt", "massacred", "definitely"	• Tentative language – "where the crime was supposed to have been committed", "I do not believe all were shot there"
• Intended audience – White Government	
• Reported speech	• Intended audience – American public
• Clearly says all were massacred in the Ipatiev House	• Direct speech
	• Innuendo or suggestion that some were killed outside the house "it is my belief they were not all killed **there**"
• Sergeyev had been sacked by this stage	• Sergeyev was still in charge of the investigation

Step 2   Can you account for the differences between these two sources?

1. Source 3 was written two (2) months later, so it is possible that Judge Sergeyev had discovered more information by the time he was sacked and therefore passed on the updated information to Judge Sokolov.

2. The reporter may have been keen to sensationalise the story by creating mystery about the whereabouts of the Czarina and children, in order to stretch out the story.

3. Judge Sergeyev, on being sacked, may have changed information in order to mislead his successor.

Observation

- Too often we are in a great hurry in our classrooms, often for reasons outside our control. When we do manage to give more time to problems and encourage learners to employ the **Comma Thinking Rule**, the resulting greater depth and breadth of thinking is most gratifying.

- I find students are amazed at what they can discover if offered the time to do so.

- Working in groups of three is highly effective.

- By praising the different perspectives raised by the students, the levels of motivation to find more differences are raised.

- This is a two-step approach. Step 1 is the analysis, whereas Step 2 asks for another level of understanding, being able to draw together evidence to suggest reasons (Comprehension) and possibilities, inferences (Synthesis).

What Happened to the Romanov Family?

Source 3
Report by Judge Sokolov who replaced Sergeyev as Chief Investigator

"My predecessor, Sergeyev, on handing the case over to me, had no doubt about the fact that the entire Romanov family had been massacred in the Ipatiev House along with those living with them. In his report...sent...on 1st February, 1919...he stated this quite definitely."

(Judge Sokolov also decided that the entire Romanov family had been killed by the Reds.)

Source 4
Report in the New York Tribune, an American newspaper, December 1918

Sergeyev took from his desk a large blue folder...and said: "Here I have all the evidence in connection with the Nicholas Romanov case...I examined the lower storey of the building where the royal family lived and where the crime was supposed to have been committed. I do not believe that all the...people, the Tsar, his family, and those with them, were shot there. It is my belief that the Empress, the Tsar's son and the four other children were not shot in that house. I believe, however, that the Tsar...the family doctor, two servants and the maid...were shot in the Ipatiev house".

SUE 1

SUE 2

K. W. L.

Topic:

What I **K**now	What I **W**ant to know	What I have **L**earnt
(Facts)	(Questions)	(• **Related Concepts**) (• **Previous Learnings**) (• **Big Picture**) (• **Metaphor**) (•**This reminds me of…**)

K.W.L. – For Thinking a Bit Deeper

This is one of the most effective strategies for engaging and motivating the learner. The acronym KWL stands for, What I Know (K), What I Want to Know (W) and What I Have Learnt (L).

This strategy is wonderful at the start of any unit, meeting or discussion. It invariably elevates thinking and discussion from the obvious and concrete to the implied, abstract and analytical. It also opens up avenues for possible investigation and the formation of hypotheses.

Topic: Bullying		
What I <u>K</u>now (K)	**What I <u>W</u>ant to Know (W)**	**What I have <u>L</u>earnt (L)**
• This is not new • There are many types of bullying, such as ... • Bullying is not restricted to schools, but is also found in ...	• Do friends of bullies really respect the bully • Can we calculate the financial costs of bullying • How can weaker people discourage the bullies	• Ego plays a large part in all types of relationships • Bullying is not restricted to the human species • Facades in buildings can cover up what lies behind, just as a bully often creates a facade

'What I Know'   Starting with what they already know makes good sense for several reasons such as showing respect to them as individuals, accessing prior knowledge, allowing mistakes, errors and misconceptions to be aired and generally building self-esteem individually and as a class as they see this column growing. Therefore, the K column is for all known or supposed facts but not opinion.

'What I Want to Know'   This is a powerful column, especially when you explain that there is no such thing as a stupid question. Also encourage students not to over-focus, but to look broader and deeper to all matters which may have impacted on the subject under review. Encourage them to be lateral, to ask awkward questions and to probe like a detective, an investigative journalist or a forensic scientist, engineer or accountant.

'What I Have Learnt'   I believe that this is the most important column. It is quite valid to simply add more information here as the course progresses, especially as a type of reflection. However, one can also use this in a more powerful way. This is the place where you challenge the learner to see the bigger picture, to see related concepts and metaphors, where you link the topic to seemingly unrelated topics or personal experiences. One could see connections between bullying and the way that certain large organisations or cartels treat smaller independent operators or how certain countries treat smaller countries. What is happening is that the learners are making sense of new topics in terms of what they already know. It is a case of dendrites (containing bits of information) joining up via a synaptic link to make more sense of their learning (and thus avoiding the danger of information being 'nonsense').

Value Add:

After completing the KWL, either individually or in small groups, through the application of a **Round Robin**, the facilitator can ask the learners to spend a few minutes ranking the data in each column in order of importance, and then invite students to offer their top ideas. The facilitator then enters this in the appropriate columns, starts a discussion and adds any points deemed to be appropriate.

What I have found to be most valuable about this strategy is that it gives the learners ownership over most of the material generated. Through ownership one achieves motivation, an important ingredient in learning success.

Applications

Use at the start of any unit, then return at several stages during a unit, then again at the end as a reflection exercise. In some classrooms, we have created a KWL on a very large sheet of paper placed on a wall with the intention of adding to it from time to time as a whole class exercise.

Try solving any problem using a KWL. Eg. My lost keys? (Template on p.60)

TOURNAMENT PRIORITISING

Kevin W McCarthy

Topic: _____

```
1. _____ ⎫
              ⎬ _____ ⎫
2. _____ ⎭           ⎬ _____ ⎫
                          ⎭           ⎬
3. _____ ⎫                       ⎬ _____ ⎫
              ⎬ _____ ⎫          ⎭           ⎬
4. _____ ⎭           ⎭                       ⎬
                                                  ⎬
5. _____ ⎫                                   ⎬
              ⎬ _____ ⎫                      ⎬
6. _____ ⎭           ⎬ _____ ⎫          ⎬
                          ⎭           ⎬          ⎬
7. _____ ⎫                       ⎬ _____⎭
              ⎬ _____ ⎫          ⎭
8. _____ ⎭           ⎭
                                                         CORE _____
9. _____ ⎫
              ⎬ _____ ⎫
10. _____ ⎭           ⎬ _____ ⎫
                          ⎭           ⎬
11. _____ ⎫                       ⎬ _____ ⎫
              ⎬ _____ ⎫          ⎭           ⎬
12. _____ ⎭           ⎭                       ⎬
                                                  ⎬
13. _____ ⎫                                   ⎬
              ⎬ _____ ⎫                      ⎬
14. _____ ⎭           ⎬ _____ ⎫          ⎬
                          ⎭           ⎬          ⎬
15. _____ ⎫                       ⎬ _____⎭
              ⎬ _____ ⎫          ⎭
16. _____ ⎭           ⎭
```

HOW?   From the list of ideas, place the 1st idea at 1, the 2nd at 16, then the
3rd idea at 5   the 4th idea at 11   the 5th idea at 2   the 6th idea at 15, and so on.

Tournament Prioritising

Kevin W McCarthy

A most useful tool to encourage rational decision making. This is based on any sporting ladder, where seeded teams struggle through the rounds for the often elusive sporting crown. As a teacher, I was involved in hockey and basketball coaching for close on twenty years and was often responsible for seeding teams and recording results. This included the 'Spoon' trophy (ie, those who were knocked out in Round 1) where teams had their own equally fierce competition in the other direction on the results board. I recently saw a version of this in 'The On-Purpose Person' (Making your life make sense) by Kevin W McCarthy. Pinon Press 1992. As a prioritising and justifying tool, it must have a place in our classrooms.

Process

1. Create a context, such as 'What do we need for survival on a tropical island in the path of cyclones?'

2. Use a Noisy Round Robin with teams of three or four students listing useful items which can be carried onto a life boat. Encourage them to list 16 items at least.

3. Then ask students to decide which is their most important item for survival (their **CORE** item)!

4. Give each group a Tournament Prioritising sheet (see page 64 for a template). The item at the top of the **Round Robin** page must be seeded No.1, the second item at No.16 (we can't have the top two seeds slugging it out in Round 1), the third item at No.2, the fourth at No.15, the fifth at No.3 and so on. Where there are two equally important items side by side on the ladder, students are permitted to make the decision to split them into the two halves so that they do not immediately eliminate each-other

5. In teams of two, three or four, decide on which items will be eliminated, and advance each 'winner' to the next round and continue until there is a winner. It is important to stress that students must 'justify' their decisions. A useful way to do that is to start the proposal with "I believe that 'a' is more important than 'b'; because ....". This is clearly higher order thinking in action, especially if it is rational and persuasive.

6. The teacher can record the ranking of all seven or eight groups on the white board and begin a general discussion and replay the Tournament Prioritiser until another **CORE** item is decided.

Observations

I have often said that the best learning and thinking takes place when the teacher is quiet, and that this depended on an interesting question, an appropriate strategy and a clear time frame. This strategy is particularly suited to this since most of the situations where students have to make decisions on the value and worth of any list is likely to be fairly personal or filled with a large degree of empathy and subjectivity.

Applications

Remember to create a large list first and the ask for the **CORE** factor

1. What is your greatest gift, attribute, privilege, value, purpose etc?

2. Which chemical is most useful to humankind in our body, our homes, in industry, in nature etc?

3. What is the greatest threat to our democratic life, our social system, our peace of mind etc?

4. What is the major factor in creating our economic position, the terrain of a particular area, the shape of 'x' etc?

In each case, Step 1 is to create a list (maybe via a Noisy Round Robin) and Step 2 is to apply the Tournament Prioritiser. Please note that the list can be from as few as four items to as many as required.

Alternative Placings

You can use another system which spreads the ideas more widely on the list. E.g.: first idea at 1, second idea at 16, third idea at 5, fourth idea at 11, fifth idea at 2, sixth idea at 15, and so on. Think about it!

Disadvantages/Improvements T Bar

Most of us are creatures of habit, to whom the expression "If you always do what you always did, you'll always get what you always got" is absolutely appropriate. If we don't notice or feel any major problems or discomfort with what we are doing, we are unlikely to challenge or question the status quo.

The '**Disadvantage/Improvements T**' strategy offers us a chance to scan our normal practices or challenge curriculum content to see if we can discover less than satisfactory situations and find solutions/improvements. We often walk around with a small pebble in our shoe and learn to curve a toe or walk on our heel to avoid the pebble. We are often too busy to stop, undo the shoe and remove the pebble. The result is a coping mentality and underperformance.

E.g.   **THE FAMILY BARBEQUE**

Disadvantages (An)	Improvements (Syn)
• Often one person does most of the work • Wood is often wet • Flies are a nuisance • Too much to do	• Decide on a 'division of labour' contract for the family • Make a wood box • Tidy garden, cover compost, plant fly repelling herbs, make a fly-screened patio, etc – eat inside • Simplify the meal, buy prepacked coleslaw, salad, etc

UMBRELLA

Disadvantages (An)	Improvements (Syn)
• Spikes can damage people's eyes • Drips on carpet/floor when used • Easy to forget/lose	• Attach rubber balls • Attach a plastic cup to end of spike, then tip out water when collected • Use a detachable wristband when starting out on the day. This wristband, worn next to your watch, will remind you that you are using an umbrella today.

Try this one.

CURRICULUM MEETINGS

Disadvantages (An)	Improvements (Syn)
•	•
•	•
•	•

——————————————————————————————

Observation

- Many people become frustrated about 'critical' and 'creative' thinking because they find it difficult to organise their thoughts. By using a simple 'T Bar' organiser, one is able to organise thoughts neatly, visibly (not just ideas floating in one's head or floating around the room via discussion) and logically, and to proceed with improvements systematically.

- This strategy often takes less than three or four minutes and, as such, is a useful tool for adding variety to the lesson and transferring the energy to the students. The recorded ideas from students, when written on the board, offer a public focus and recognition of their ideas. As such, it is a motivational strategy.

- So much of what happens in schools on a daily basis could be subjected to the quick scrutiny of the **Disadvantages/Improvements T**. Create a list of daily tasks, events, occurrences and either on your own or with one or more colleagues, apply the **Disadvantages/Improvements T** to ascertain how you can remove the pebbles from your shoe so that you can spend more time on the creative part of teaching – good lesson preparation!!

- Allied to this is the **Important/Unimportant 'T'**. Laurie Keim and Peter Hartshorn, two excellent Brisbane teachers, have a mythical junk box to which is assigned any job which they feel is not important. This allows them to get on with their core business – lesson preparation and exciting teaching.

Remember

It may not
be broken

BUT

How could it be
EVEN
BETTER?

Eric Frangenheim, Rodin Educational Consultancy ©

SUE 1 _____

_____

_____

_____

_____

SUE 2 _____

_____

_____

_____

_____

Eric Frangenheim, Rodin Educational Consultancy © Ⓟ

DECISION MAKING MATRIX

Topic:

Criteria Value 1–5									Total
A									
B									
C									

CRITICAL ANALYSIS

Eric Frangenheim ©

The Decision Making Matrix
(also described as Table Construction)

This incorporates **Criteria**, **Value** and **Round Robin**, and is useful in making decisions on comparable items or proposals.

Process for teaching this strategy to learners

Step 1   Draw a simple matrix as below and ask the students which house would be the best to buy, A, B or C.

	£k	
House A	100	
House B	120	
House C	150	

Some answers and resulting discussion will lead to the comment that price alone cannot lead to a wise decision.

Step 2   The teacher could then ask what else could be used to help make a decision, and record two or three of these on the board, e.g., location, number of rooms, age of building. A '**Round Robin**' can now be employed with learners in groups of 3–6, asking them to think of other 'things' to consider. Give approximately 30 seconds between each shift of paper. Then ask each group what these 'things' could be called, and invariably the word 'criteria' will emerge. The class teacher can have a brief discussion as to why this is important in decision making. Next, ask each group to select the ten most important criteria or factors in deciding which house to buy, and transfer some from each group to the matrix on the board.

Buying a Home

Criteria →	£K	Resale Position	Age	Number of Bedrooms	Lock-up Garage	Crime in Area	Proximity to Public Transport	Quality of Air	Etc.
A	100	Excellent	40 years	3	No	Low	Train & Bus	Fair	
B	120	Questionable	6 years	4	Yes	Fairly high	Bus	Very good	
C	150	Stable	1 year	5	2 garages Yes	Low	Train & Bus	Excellent	

This is a two-step operation:

Step 3   is filling in the 10 factors along the top line. Insert the term 'Criteria' above House A, indicating that these are the factors to be considered. Relative information will be entered in the boxes below.

Step 4   constitutes the **Remember–Analyse** process in terms of Bloom's Taxonomy (Cognitive). The information can be gained from brochures, advertisements and telephone calls

The teacher could then stand back from the board, congratulate the students, and ask them now to make a decision. After some discussion, students are likely to comment that there is too much information and that it is now too difficult to make a decision.

Step 5 The next step is to introduce them to the idea of assigning a value to each cell using a 1–5 scale, five (5) being most important and one (1) being least important; and ask the students, either individually or in small groups, to decide on the comparable rating of each column. For example, if your priority is to save money, House A would rate a 5, B a 4 and C a 3 or 2 or even 1.

Ask students to assign Values dealing with one column or Criteria at a time, and then total each row.

Buying a Home

Criteria → Value ↓	£K	Resale Position	Age	Number of Bedrooms	Lock-up Garage	Crime in Area	Proximity to Public Transport	Quality of Air	Etc.	Total
A	5 100	5 Excellent	1 40 years	3 3	0 No	5 Low	4 Train & Bus	3 Fair		26
B	4 120	2 Questionable	4 6 years	4 4	4 Yes	2 Fairly high	2 Bus	4 Very good		26
C	3 150	4 Stable	5 1 year	5 5	5 2 garages Yes	5 Low	5 Ferry, Train & Bus	5 Excellent		37

As a result of assigning Values, it is clear that House C is the preferred option.

The whole process of the Decision Making Matrix employs several levels of Bloom's Taxonomy (Cognitive), such as:
- **Remember/Understand** and **Apply** (the data in the squares or cells)
- **Analyse** – each Criteria
- **Evaluate** – rating the Value of the comparable data.

This strategy can be termed a form of **Critical Analysis**.

What if?

- A student asks whether it is fair that all factors have the same rating values (1-5)? You can open this up for discussion. The consensus invariably is that not all factors are of equal value. The next avenue is to ask, "What should we do about it?" Again, the discussion invariably leads to the decision to double (6-10) or treble (11-15) the values.
- A student comments that different people have different ideas on a) the factors to be used; and, b) the actual rating of each comparable factor? You can open this to discussion (maybe by using a **Think:Pair:Share**), with the likely consensus being that this is true and reflects the value of differences.

What next?

Next ask students to draw up a simple matrix to decide on a process for choosing a pair of jeans.

Criteria →	Cost £	Brand	Shop	Colour				Total
A	30							
B	40							
C	50							

Students could work in pairs and attempt to decide which factors to consider. Ask for some feed back.

What next?

Ask students to list other issues where the Decision Making Matrix could be used.

E.g., Choosing:

- Holiday venues

- Career choices

- Universities

- Car

- Computer

- Marriage partner

- The most effective poem, literacy work, television drama, etc

- Australian of the Year

- Monarchy or Republic

Observation

- Decision making can lead to positive or disastrous consequences. Bad decisions are usually the result of impatience and lack of organisation of data. For this reason, teaching students to use the **Decision Making Matrix** may save them from future personal problems and will also help them to be better thinkers.

- Parents who encourage their children to complete the **Decision Making Matrix** with them in order to make family-based decisions will find they are creating the thinking family with greater bonding.

- Good thinking does not happen automatically, but is rather the result of a process. The **Decision Making Matrix** is a longer process, but is well worth the time.

- Some teachers are using this strategy as the major focus of assignments.

Note:

On page 72 there is a sheet that I present at my Thinking Strategies Workshops, showing how I can use a **Decision Making Matrix** as the exit point for a unit of work such as Nutrition for Busy People. I use the **Decision Making Matrix** for this analytical and decision making process when I start with the 'end in mind' and design an assessment item which asks students to compare and contrast and then select the best of two or three choices. This is particularly useful if I insist they employ the **Decision Making Matrix** framework for their initial research and thinking, and that they use the various criteria as paragraphs to help them structure their final report. I would also insist (or is it suggest these days) that they submit the **Decision Making Matrix** with their final written report as this would help me to see their thinking and how they have reached their final conclusion..

SUE 1

SUE 2

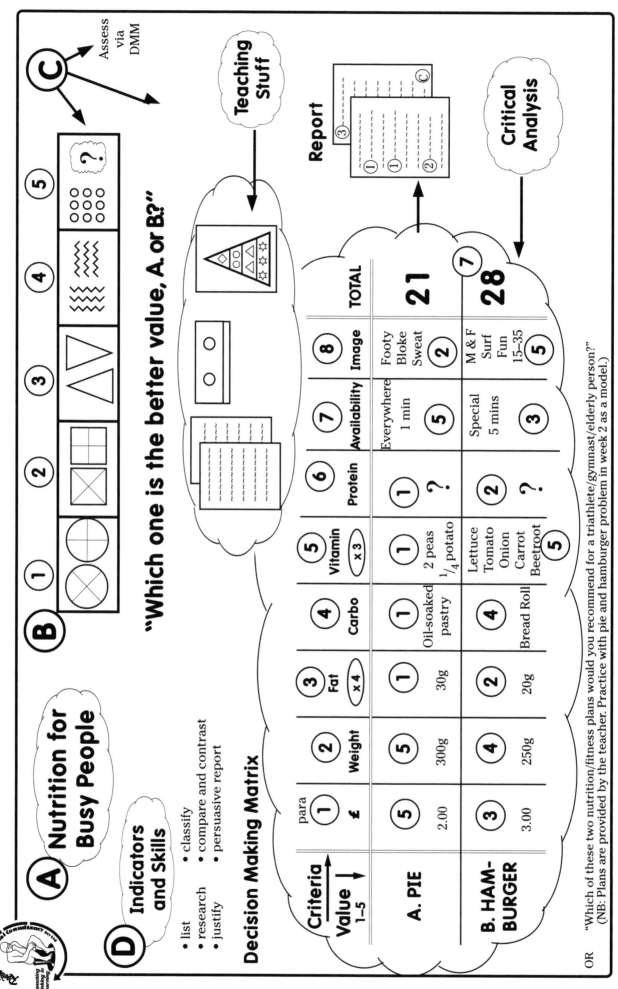

A Nutrition for Busy People

D Indicators and Skills
- list
- research
- justify
- classify
- compare and contrast
- persuasive report

Decision Making Matrix

B 1 2 3 4 5

"Which one is the better value, A or B?"

Teaching Stuff

C → Assess via DMM

Report

Critical Analysis

Criteria Value 1–5	para ① £	② Weight	③ Fat (x4)	④ Carbo	⑤ Vitamin (x3)	⑥ Protein	⑦ Availability	⑧ Image	TOTAL
A. PIE	⑤ 2.00	⑤ 300g	① 30g	① Oil-soaked pastry	① 2 peas 1/4 potato	① ?	Everywhere 1 min ⑤	Footy Bloke Sweat ②	**21**
B. HAM-BURGER	③ 3.00	④ 250g	② 20g	④ Bread Roll	Lettuce Tomato Onion Carrot Beetroot ⑤	② ?	Special 5 mins ③	M & F Surf Fun 15–35 ⑤	**28** ⑦

OR "Which of these two nutrition/fitness plans would you recommend for a triathlete/gymnast/elderly person?" (NB: Plans are provided by the teacher. Practice with pie and hamburger problem in week 2 as a model.)

Creative Thinking

Too often as teachers, we expect our charges to be creative without offering a creative thinking strategy.

We use terms such as "Put on your thinking cap" or "Let your creative juices flow", etc.

Now, it is true that all of us have natural creativity and have a range of personal experiences to draw on. However, as mentioned earlier in this book, it is not particularly fair to ask students to be creative without offering a few tools.

Consider the feelings of failure students will and do experience when they observe others generating creative ideas while their own sheets are blank. Experiencing failure several times is enough to persuade most of us that we simply are 'not creative' (the converse of the Success Spiral). I am dismayed at the large number of teachers, parents and students who often state that they are not creative.

Creativity, by the very nature of the topic, will have thousands of definitions, so I will certainly not offer any definitive statement. However, I believe that creativity is to do with a perceived problem or need, the confidence to believe one can address that problem or need, the ability to look for the component parts of that problem (**Remember**, **Apply** and **Analyse**), and the ability to bring one's world view and experiences to generate one or more ideas (**Create**). So Creativity has a Process and a Product (without any need for perfection in the early stage).

The next few chapters offer several strategies which may help your students with Creativity.

- **SCAMPER**
- **Word Association**
- **MASC**
- **Forced Relations**
- **Encouraging Lateral Thinking**

If you always
DO
What you always
DID
You'll always
GET
What you always
GOT!!

A reason to Reassess?

Rodin Educational Consultancy ©

SCAMPER
(Bob Eberle)

This is a useful strategy to generate new or alternative ideas. It is a creative/divergent /design thinking tool. It can be used in many situations such as asking students to re-write the story of Goldilocks and the Three Bears.

SCAMPER is an acronym:

S...Substitute. A person, place, time or situation.
e.g., What do you think would have happened if there had been a crazy scientist bear instead of Father Bear?

C...Combine. Blend assorted ideas, situation, materials.
e.g., What could have happened if the three bears were having a family reunion with relatives who had escaped from a zoo where they had been badly treated by the zoo keepers?

A...Adapt. Or adjust to suit a purpose.
e.g., How might the story have changed if Goldilocks had one leg in a plaster cast and was using crutches?

M...Modify. By making some of the features larger or smaller and changing the number of times something happens.
e.g., What would have happened if the Bears were much smaller than Goldilocks?

P...Put the original intention or some part of the story to other use.
e.g., What if Goldilocks was only pretending to be lost and was really looking for an excuse to go into other people's houses?

E...Eliminate any feature or part.
e.g., How could the story change if there was no Father Bear?

R...Rearrange or reverse the sequence or order or positioning of the item under review.
e.g., Retell the story so that it is Baby Bear who is lost and goes into the house of Goldilocks' parents.

Observation

- Many people claim that they are not creative, yet when supplied with this strategy, they are soon able to debunk that contention.

- Though the Goldilocks example was quite frivolous, a Scamper can be used to generate new ideas for your teaching practice, the way you present or revise lessons, apply discipline, reorganise and reinvigorate your academic department or faculty, think about improving a school assembly or running any school function. It can also be used when assessing personal relationships with a view to improving one that is strained.

- One does not necessarily have to go through all seven steps, but may simply use four or five.

SUE 1 _____

SUE 2 _____

WORD ASSOCIATION
The 'Ideas' Launch Pad

Too often students complain that they are not creative. Too often we use previous ideas as so called 'creative ideas'. This strategy helps learners to generate new ideas or solutions via associations with a chosen launch pad word or object.

The 'Launch Pad' word or object will help get students out of their usual thinking patterns.

Process

Step 1   Decide on the object or subject for which you need new ideas or solutions. For example, a better toothbrush for the 21st Century or to encourage children to brush their teeth.

Step 2   Think of a word or object which has nothing to do with the topic needing new ideas, such as a 'wrist watch'. Place this in the middle of a page on the **launch pad**. Students use their imagination to think of associated words, opposites, puns, etc. This continues until they think of an idea.

Place a ❑ (box) around this idea. Students then start again at the **launch pad word** and look for more associations until they get more ideas. Students can also start from one of the words in an association link. Students should give their brains permission to be silly, exciting, different, even a bit crazy.

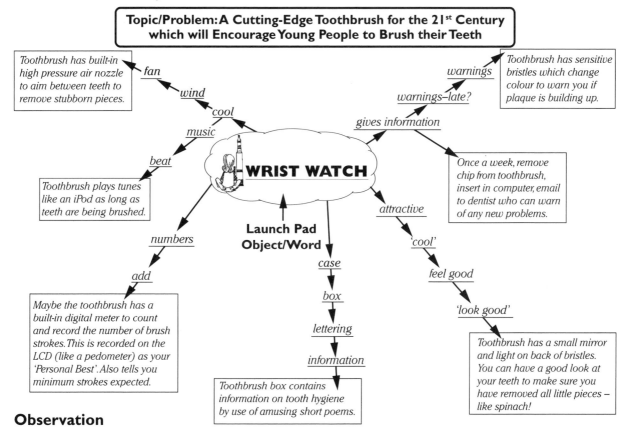

Topic/Problem: A Cutting-Edge Toothbrush for the 21ˢᵗ Century which will Encourage Young People to Brush their Teeth

Toothbrush has built-in high pressure air nozzle to aim between teeth to remove stubborn pieces.

fan — *wind* — *cool* — *music* — *beat*

Toothbrush plays tunes like an iPod as long as teeth are being brushed.

numbers — *add*

Maybe the toothbrush has a built-in digital meter to count and record the number of brush strokes. This is recorded on the LCD (like a pedometer) as your 'Personal Best'. Also tells you minimum strokes expected.

WRIST WATCH

Launch Pad Object/Word

case — *box* — *lettering* — *information*

Toothbrush box contains information on tooth hygiene by use of amusing short poems.

gives information — *warnings* — *warnings–late?*

Toothbrush has sensitive bristles which change colour to warn you if plaque is building up.

Once a week, remove chip from toothbrush, insert in computer, email to dentist who can warn of any new problems.

attractive — *'cool'* — *feel good* — *'look good'*

Toothbrush has a small mirror and light on back of bristles. You can have a good look at your teeth to make sure you have removed all little pieces – like spinach!

Observation

This strategy is also very useful for creative writing. Think of a topic or theme, find a **launch word**, and zoom ahead with ideas.

SUE 1 _____

SUE 2 _____

M.A.S.C.
(Gerard Alford)

MASC is an effective creative tool that assists students with *design* tasks, such as redesigning everyday products, familiar stories or pieces of music. The acronym represents:

M Modify
A Add
S Size
C Change

Process

This strategy can be used for students to undertake individually – but it is highly recommended as a small group cooperative task, as students tend to generate more creative ideas in a shorter time through team work.

The steps involved are:

Step 1: **Modify:** Modify a feature or replace one part with another.
Step 2: **Add:** Add a new feature to the object.
Step 3: **Size:** Make one part or several parts of the object bigger and/or smaller.
Step 4: **Change:** This could involve changing the shape, texture, colour or ergonomics.

If students were required to redesign a product, such as a toothbrush, the MASC strategy could be employed:

Modify The bristles are replaced with pads, for better cleaning and longevity.

Add The inside of the handle stores the toothpaste. This allows a free-flow system, where the toothpaste automatically flows down the inside of the handle onto the brush, ready for cleaning the teeth.

Size Make the handle longer so that it fits comfortably in the hand.

Change Change the shape of the handle so that it is concave. This enables to establish a better grip for the user.

MASC can be applied to stories as well as objects:

M Replace a character or an event with another. (Modify)
A Add another character into the story (Add)
S Rewrite the story so that one character becomes more important (Size)
C Change the ending or the setting (Change)

Observation

Creating a new product or an original story can be very difficult for some students. The concept of redesigning an everyday product or rewriting a familiar story using the MASC strategy is far less threatening and could be an end task in itself, or as a means of moving students towards original design work.

Applications

Primary: Middle: Creative Writing (English)

MASC a well known favourite story.
Modify   the setting.
Add   a new character.
Size   the character so that it/he/she has a bigger role.
Change   the ending by extending it.

Junior: School Assembly

Modify   the order of events.
Add   music and colour.
Size   students have a greater role.
Change   the location of the next assembly.

Secondary: Redesigning Games (PE)

Use MASC to modify the rules of a game, such as tennis, to make it easier for beginners.
Modify   the serving position so it is close to the net.
Add   another bounce – the ball can bounce twice.
Size   the court area to include the doubles area.
Change   the height of the net by lowering it.

Macroeconomic Policy (Economics)

Use MASC to analyse changes in economic policy settings.
Modify   inflation stability to hyperinflation.
Add   an external shock, eg the oil crisis.
Size   interest rates to twice present rate.
Change   the Government.

Forced Relationships

I first came upon this strategy as a six year-old attending boarding school in Holland. On Saturday afternoons and evenings we played games or were involved in activities. One of them was a type of **forced relationships** by which we were given four or five unconnected items, some from the forest such as bark, grass, twigs, leaves and items of clothing or items from our desk. Most of us would have different stimulus material and would be given five to ten minutes to create an imaginative story from ideas associated with the forced relationships. I remember that this brought out the best in some students and caused great hilarity.

The real use of the **Forced Relationships** is in every-day problem solving and in creative writing.

Problems which teachers often face include unmotivated students. How would an eraser, a toothbrush and a lettuce help you improve the atmosphere?

The eraser may help you decide to forget the past; the toothbrush may encourage you to redecorate your classroom to give it a different feel; and the lettuce, which is to do with healthy living, may result in a decision to encourage yourself and your students to notice all the positives which occur in the learning process and to reward these developments in word and deed. The overall package you are creating is an amalgam of all three items.

Observation

Teachers will need to believe in the value of encouraging different thinking. Students very soon detect whether or not teachers are sincere about creative thinking. By not assigning negative comments to their responses, we are more likely to produce creative thinkers.

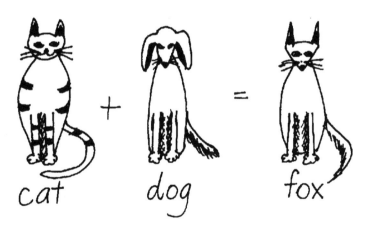

cat + dog = fox

☝ **SUE 1**

☝ **SUE 2**

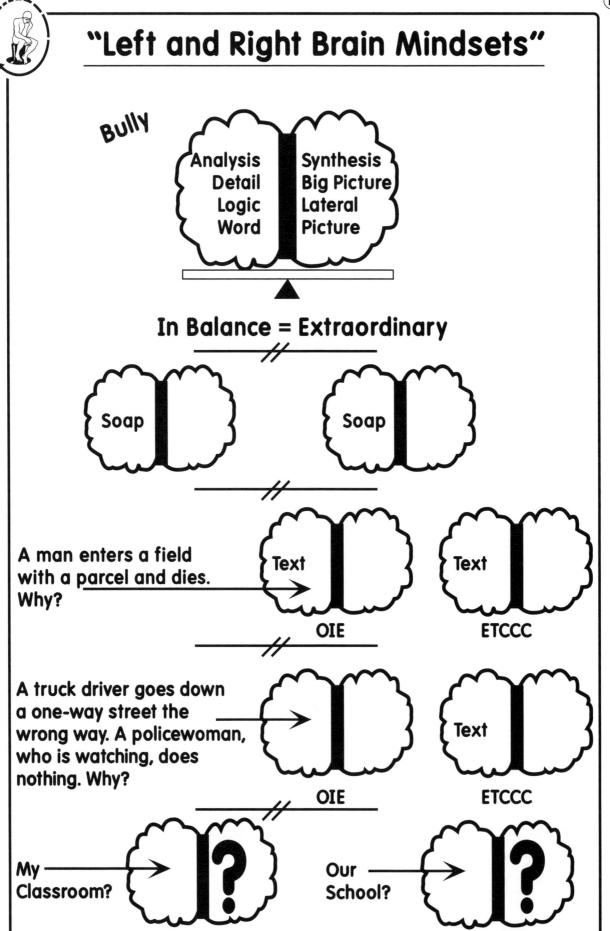

Encouraging Lateral Thinking

Too often we encourage learners to be more lateral in their thinking, more lateral in their creativity, without really explaining how to be lateral. I certainly make no claim to expertise in this area, but do offer the following process to allow learners to be more in touch with creative thinking.

Please refer to the illustration opposite.

I discuss some basic differences in types of thinking, which are sometimes explained as differences in left and right brain thinking. Left brain thinking tends to be more analytical, searching for details, more minute in its gaze, dependent on literal meaning, logical and highly definitional. On the other hand, right brain thinking is characterised by the big picture, more holistic in nature, synthesising, creating ideas and is dependent more on pictures than words and prefers colours. It is also the lateral thinking rather than logical thinking part of our operation.

I also explain that much of what we visualise (often regarded as right brained) is highly governed by the literal and definitional left brain.

Let me explain. If I say the word "soap", the analytical, definitional cognitive process tends to create a picture of a bar of soap. This is usually correct, especially since most of us are programmed along the "If you always do what you always did, you'll always get what you always got" paradigm. So logically soap refers to a bar of soap, but lateral thinkers may well conjure up images of soap operas instead.

If I were to say "fire engine", ninety-nine percent would visualise a red fire fighting lorry rather than a car engine or swimming pool motor on fire. The reason for this is that **we are the sum total of our experiences**, and unless we regularly **wish** to break the mould of orthodoxy and conventionality, we won't. The fact is that left brain thinking tends to dominate most of us past the age of 6–8.

So how do we train ourselves to be more lateral and less logical when the situation demands it? One simple and effective way is to work with **lateral thinking**™ problems such as those in Paul Sloan's books.

I explain that Rule No.1, Rule No.2, etc is to be aware of the assumption/s and to challenge the assumption/s.

When I ask students to solve the following problem:

"A man enters a field with a parcel and dies. Why?"

(I can only answer *yes* or *no*)

The types of logical answers they offer could include:

- He had a heart attack
- The parcel was a bomb/was toxic/held a snake which bit him/was a poisoned hamburger, etc
- He entered a minefield/battlefield/electrified field
- He died of old age

  and many other perfectly sensible answers, which in this case are all wrong.

I then ask my audience to shut their eyes, hold on to their right ear (the switch or dial to their right brain) and say the following words:

"Right brain, I give you permission to change the picture"

Keeping their eyes closed, I repeat the problem *"A man enters a field, carrying a parcel, and dies"*. I ask them to be aware of the picture of the action which the analytical, definitional left brain is sending to the right brain. Most people see the man walking into the field or climbing over a gate or fence. I then ask them to give their right ear a twist and change the picture by seeing his direction of entry in a totally different, even ludicrous, direction. Within seconds the arms go up, and most get the answer, which is:

"He was a parachutist whose parachute (the parcel) failed to open"

Topic:

The point is that here **lateral thinkers challenged the assumption**, which is that he entered the field in the normal way (just as soap is normally seen as a bar of soap) and decided to see the problem in a lateral way.

The next problem is as follows.

> *"A truck driver goes down a one-way street the wrong way.*
> *A policewoman is watching but does not stop him. Why?"*

Logically, the driver should be fined, but if he is not fined, then there must be another scenario. So learners close their eyes, listen to the words, and soon realise that the pictorial definition of a truck driver is that of a person driving a truck. Changing the picture, they soon emerge with a truck driver *walking* down the street, and therefore not doing anything illegal.

A third problem is as follows.

> *"A cowgirl rides her horse into town on Friday, has a wonderful weekend and*
> *leaves immediately after the weekend on Wednesday. How is this possible?"*

If we use analytical left brain thinking, we soon realise that the problem lies with the word Wednesday since it is not logical for Wednesday to follow immediately after a weekend. Close your eyes. How do you normally see Wednesday – the answer is that it is a day of the week. So twist your ear to change it so that it is no longer a day of the week and it becomes the name of the cowgirl's horse!!

This is obviously not a scientific explanation of lateral thinking, but it works for me and many others. The point is that it is so easy to be ordinary (see page 119 **OIE-ETCCC**), but to be outside the ordinary takes creativity, courage and commitment. In terms of creativity, being prepared to see things differently is essential, and one way is to use our *intrapersonal intelligence*, to be aware of our thinking and assumptions and to be prepared to challenge these assumptions and to create alternative realities.

The point is clear. The left brain, our conventional way of thinking, can be a bit of a bully. However, we can be in charge of our thinking and that is a fairly exciting idea!!!

Challenge!

How to join all nine dots with straight lines. You may not move your pen off the paper once you start.

5 straight lines *(easy)*	**4 straight lines**	**3 straight lines**	**1 straight line**
• • • • • • • • •	• • • • • • • • •	• • • • • • • • •	• • • • • • • • •
	'Tip': Think outside the square	Use a KWL	Challenge the dimension assumption

SUE 1 _____

SUE 2 _____

Y Chart and Creative Writing

I have worked at Rutherglen Primary School in Northern Victoria on three occasions in 2003 and 2004. It is truly an inspiring learning environment with a motivated staff and delightful students. In one of the Year two classes, I designed a 90 minute lesson with teachers Julie Bowers, Kylie Weekes and Tim Courtis. The lesson was on 'The Sun' and one of the activities called for some creative writing. I made a rather rough drawing of a 4WD vehicle stuck in the forbidding desert, with footmarks leading away. (My son-in-law, Mick Powell has created this more respectable cartoon below.)

The Y chart produced wonderful responses, including:
- 'foolish parents for leaving the vehicle' and 'water in radiator' (looks like)
- "are we going to live?", 'flapping of vulture wings' (sounds like)
- 'dusty', 'thirsty', 'scared', 'guilty' (the parents), 'alone' (feels like)

We then introduced a game ranger by drawing him into the left hand side of the picture and continued drawing more responses on the Y Chart. The third complication was the introduction of a hungry lion between the ranger and the distant hillock behind which the family had disappeared. One student pointed out that the people must still be alive, using the circling eagles as her evidence and so the tension was built up. Could the ranger get to them in time before the lion?

Once the white board was full of brainstormed material, we played some Bach and asked the students to write a story, with the suggestion that they use some of the material on the white board. I was amazed to note that several students had no trouble writing as much as three pages for their stories. All students were well focussed and obviously enjoyed the experience. It made me realise once again the value of ownership in motivating students, for after all, nearly everything that was on the white board was theirs!!!

The Power of Three (Cooperative Strategies)

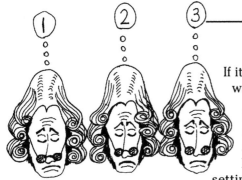

If it is true that no person is an island we may need to look at the way we organise our classrooms from time to time.

For twelve years of schooling, I sat behind other boys and regularly noticed the **dandruff** in their hair and on their collars and shirts. On reflection, I realise that looking at the backs of hair and at dandruff was probably not the most inspiring setting for thinking creatively or critically. For the first twelve years of my own teaching (four years at university had not offered any alternatives) I subjected my own students to the 'dandruff regime' before I was introduced to some cooperative settings.

It was in 1990 that I first met Joan Dalton. The ten G & T education advisers were involved in the annual one week inservice in Brisbane and Joan was the facilitator for several of those days. She dealt with the effectiveness of cooperative thinking strategies and inspired us to allow students to do the thinking. Not just gifted students benefit from this style of teaching, all students benefit from these cooperative strategies.

The cooperative learning movement has done a great deal in the past ten to fifteen years to impress upon teachers the value of harnessing the synergy produced by group work. Cooperative learning is not about putting learners into groups and asking them to discuss a topic. If anything it may well be an invitation to create mayhem. Useful group work depends on clear instructions and clear roles for learners in a group. As I have mentioned elsewhere, the best learning takes place when the teacher is quiet but this depends on a useful activity, an appropriate strategy and a time frame. For example, students may be placed in groups of three and asked to use the **Y Chart** to analyse a painting or document and be asked to employ the **Silent Round Robin**. This is more likely to set up the class for success than simply ask them to sit in groups and discuss the picture.

Over the next few pages, I wish to share with you some of those strategies which I use regularly in my teaching. These are:

- **Round Robin** (Noisy and Quiet)

- **Hot Potato**

- **Jigsaw**

- **Doughnut** or **Inner-Outer Circle**

- **Triad**

- **Think: Pair: Share**

- **1: 4: Publish: Circle: Refine**

- **Think: Whisper: Repeat: Share**

- **Pairs and RAS Alert**

"The Dandruff Regime"

Round Robin

This is one of the most effective strategies for cooperative learning. It avoids several of the disadvantages of a whole-class brainstorm and is highly synergistic. The **Round Robin** is a valuable strategy at the start of any unit since it allows the teacher to discover the general level of knowledge of the class and can also be used for revision purposes, as well as being used for specific purposes. It takes some organising and is best practised in a non-threatening or non-curricular setting. For example, the class may be asked to think of all the alternative uses of a rubber thong. (I saw the results of this challenge from students at Alexander Bay State School in the Daintree Forest. They were highly unusual such as "a tongue depressor for a sick giant".)

There are two types of **Round Robin – Quiet** and **Noisy**. The **Quiet** Round Robin will be dealt with in the process below.

Process for the Quiet Round Robin

1. Split the class into groups of 3–6 students. Each student is to have a response sheet and a pen/pencil.

2. Each student is given the same problem or task; e.g., to list alternative uses for rubber thongs.

3. At a given signal, every learner begins to write responses on their own piece of paper. No talking takes place. After one to two minutes, give a signal (*Yoplait* – see below) to change sheets. Each student passes their paper to the person on their left, reads the new sheet, and then continues to write more ideas on that piece of paper but may not repeat what was written on the first paper and may not repeat what has just been read.

4. Repeat the swapping of response sheets until one's own sheet is returned or until ideas dry up. This occurs every 30 seconds to two minutes or longer, depending on the question and level of consideration.

5. Each group can then discuss their findings, make a collated report on a large piece of paper and report back on the best one, two, three or four ideas.

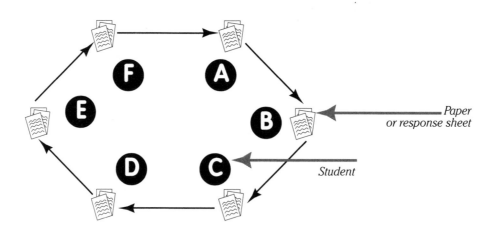

Paper or response sheet

Student

Observation

- The strength of the Round Robin is that no one person can dominate the thinking of others. Furthermore, when one dries out of ideas, reading someone else's tends to stimulate new ideas through piggy backing.

- The major benefit is that whereas in a whole-group brainstorm only one person is responding, in a Round Robin, every student is on task at all times.

- Shyer students are more at ease in this situation as they are not visible.

- Less confident students often find that ideas they have generated have also been offered by others. This serves as affirmation that their ideas are possibly better than they would normally admit.

- There is a tacit understanding that each student needs to contribute to avoid letting down the team.

- A large range of ideas can be generated rapidly.

- By asking groups to select the two or three most important, unusual, significant responses and then transferring these to the board, students are engaging in higher order thinking (evaluation) and are motivated by seeing their ideas displayed publicly. By asking students to select the best two or three ideas in their group, we are encouraging them to honour the ideas of others and to be objective – both of which are socially necessary behaviours.

- This is a useful strategy for families.

- In terms of Bloom's Taxonomy:

  a) The Round Robin can be used to generate information or data (**Remember**), look for meanings (**Understand**) and look for uses (**Apply**)

  b) At a higher order thinking level, the Round Robin can:
     i. be linked to a **Pros:Cons:Questions**, **SWOT** Analysis or **Y Chart** to complete an **Analysis** of a topic
     ii. linked to a **Random Input** or **Scamper** and the **Y Chart** to generate new ideas (**Create**)
     iii. linked to a **Pros:Cons:Questions**, **Y Chart** and **Decision Making Matrix** to assist in an **Evaluation** exercise.

Yoplait

I explain to my students that *Yoplait* is French for *Yum, Yoghurt* and is also French for "*Pay Attention*" or in this case it means "*Finish the sentence and pass the sheet to the next person or group in a clockwise direction*". It is simply a signal in my class that the exercise is to end.

The Noisy Round Robin

This is similar to the Quiet Round Robin but what is different is that there is talking since each group has only one response sheet and one scribe. At the command to pass on the piece of paper (*Yoplait*) after the first minute or so, each group passes the paper to the table to their left, and the normal Round Robin rules apply. This creates great energy in the class. This is an excellent strategy for staff meetings.

SUE 1 _____

_____
_____
_____
_____

SUE 2 _____

_____
_____
_____
_____

Hot Potato

This is another excellent form of **Brainstorming** in a cooperative setting. It is very similar to a **Round Robin** but whereas a Round Robin gives every group the same problem or question, in a **Hot Potato**, each group or station has a different problem or question or sub topic which is part of the umbrella topic. Note that since a hot potato can only be held for a short time, The **Hot Potato** strategy is similarly a rapidly moving exercise. In this case, the pieces of paper are the hot potatoes.

Process

1. Divide the class into groups of 3-6 students. Each group is to have a large sheet of paper and one pen or pencil.
2. Each group is given a different problem to solve, which can be sub-topics of one problem. The problem is to be written clearly at the top of the sheet. At a given signal, each group begins to discuss their problem, with one person writing down the responses or ideas.
3. After a period of time a signal is given by the teacher *(Yoplait)* then each sheet is moved to the table on the left. In this manner, each group now receives a different problem to address.
4. Each group now reads and clarifies the new problem or topic, reads the responses on the sheet, and continues to discuss the problem. As ideas flow, they are written on the sheet.
5. Repeat the swapping process until each group has dealt with each problem.
6. The results can be posted on the wall for all to study and/or a general discussion can take place based on all the information generated. A more organised process may be to give all sheets to a smaller group which is given the brief to put together a final report containing a solution or a series of solutions.

Observation

- Though this strategy can take up a certain amount of time, the chances are that the benefits far outweigh the disadvantages. I find that most/all students are on task for most/all of the process, and that there is a great sense of being valued and trusted. I have used this at leadership camps with groups as large as 120 students who were attempting to generate ideas and policies to improve the functioning of their school. There is a distinct air of ownership in this strategy.

- The Hot Potato described above is the noisy version because each group is talking with one scribe per group recording the ideas which are generated. The quiet version is when the size of each group is determined by the number of sub-topics. For example, if we are to discuss an umbrella topic which has four sub-topics, we will have four students in each group. Each student will be given one of the sub-topics and deals with that one until the signal is given to pass the sheet to the left. Obviously, no talking takes place and as a result, this is the silent **Hot Potato**.

- The information generated from the **Hot Potato** can be used in a variety of ways.

SUE I	SUE 2

Example

An example of an Umbrella Problem is 'How to Create the Thinking School'. Sub Topics could include:

a) Role of Principal and Senior Administration

b) Role of Heads of Faculty (High Schools)

c) What does the Staff Room/Common Room look like? What happens here?

d) Physical make up of School (School Environment) – buildings, signs, notice boards, newsletters, etc.

Sub-Topic 1:   Role of Senior Administration

- Encourage *professional development* and attendance by staff
- Implement system to spread important/relevant *information* to all staff
- Put emphasis on academic and other activities, not just sport
- Take on thinking strategies and *practise* them at staff meetings i.e. do C.P.S. to evaluate/get new ideas, etc
- Invite *inspiring* professional development people to staff meetings
- Fight for more *T.R.S. (Teacher Relief Scheme) time* so that teachers are able to attend professional development workshops, seminars
- Encourage *interaction* with other staff to appreciate role of all members on staff and more importantly between students

Sub-Topic 2:   Staff Room/Common Room

- Bright positive decor
- Good facilities
- Availability of staff to students and a foyer/area for students to approach staff (friendly) so students aren't intimidated
- Librarian compiles and distributes list of useful Gifted and Talented and other literature to staff
- Wall charts on various thinking strategies
- Graffiti board for written comments
- Peer inservice about useful strategies

Sub-Topic 3:   Classrooms

- Visual prompts like **Y Chart**, **brainstorming guides** displayed around room
- Seating arrangements – grouping rather than rows
- Providing space to take time out to learn autonomously
- Individual education programs/research projects geared at interest of students
- Facility to allow child to leave classroom (to library, etc) to produce personal project
- Bright colours
- Student projects displayed and rotated regularly
- Access to computer resource facilities
- Taught by guest lecturers
- Giving students time to do things
- Develop responsibility in the students for independent and active learning
- Value originality

Sub-Topic 4: School Environment

- Lots of trees and greenery
- Murals and graffiti constructively done by students
- Lots of colours
- Public recognition at assemblies of academic/thinking activities and achievements
- Student performances at assembly, e.g. talks, plays, music, reports of activities
- Run competitions to encourage thinking skills at assemblies
- T.O.M. and other G & T initiatives
- Form Thinkers Club and Thinkers' Club facilitator to work in classrooms
- Problem Solving strategies to be worked into C.C.P.s or Work Programs and Units
- Encourage parent involvement in activities like Thinkers Club and T.O.M.
- Reports home about Thinking initiatives present in individual classrooms
- Strategies which can be used at home sent home to parents
- Report on achievement of students' efforts, not performances
- Invites for parent speakers
- Tap into parent 'expertise' with articles of interest
- Publish newspaper reports
- Cryptic words, signs on doors
- Outdoor chess
- Avoid straight paths – use curves

Note: The results from this **Hot Potato** are taken from one of my teacher in-service sessions in 1997

SUE I _____

_____
_____
_____

SUE 2 _____

_____
_____
_____

Jigsaw
(Spencer Kagan)

This is a useful strategy enabling a group of learners to cover several topics simultaneously and in a shorter amount of time. The learners move from their **home group** to what are designated 'expert groups' and then back to their **home group**.

Process

The number of topics which can be dealt with equals the number of learners in each Home Group, ie, if you have groups of four, then four topics can be covered. These groups are known as **Home Groups**.

1. Offer four topics to be dealt with in depth.
   If we took the case of formulating a plan to create the Thinking School, we might decide to tackle this proposal under four headings, viz:
   a) how to create the thinking classroom
   b) how to create the thinking staffroom and thinking faculties
   c) the role of HOFs and SACs and Director of Academics
   d) changes to curriculum, assessment and reporting.
      Each of these topics is designated as an **Expert Group** centre. Therefore only four tables will be used, and some learners will have to take a chair to these **Expert Groups**.

2. The four people in each **Home Group** are to decide which of the four topics each would like to discuss in the **Expert Group**. Each member of the Home Group must go to a different **Expert Group**.

3. Within each **Expert Group**, in-depth discussions now take place on that topic. Notes should be taken. At the conclusion of this session, a Round Robin can be conducted within the Expert Group, recording what has been said, so that each person can take a record of the deliberations to their Home Group. This session can last for five to ten minutes or longer.

4. Learners now return to their **Home Group** where each person in turn reports back on the findings of the **Expert Group** and attempts to 'sell' the ideas gained in that **Expert Group**. A final report is collated. Modifications can be made by the other members of the Home Group

5. Each **Home Group** then presents their report to the whole class.

SUE 1 _____

SUE 2 _____

Observation

- This strategy takes some time to explain and organise. However, it allows students to cover a great deal of information in a relatively short period of time and encourages communication skills.

- Each group can be charged with preparing a group presentation in a variety of ways. This again encourages group problem solving. It also allows those learners who do not operate well in larger groups the opportunity to feel less threatened.

- This is a lively and at times noisy strategy, but then good teachers can always distinguish between on-task and off-task noise!

Applications

1. Planning a school fete where the Expert Groups would each be discussing a sub section of the fete.

2. Studying educational or syllabus documents at a staff meeting.

3. Studying stimulus materials which may be of a lengthy nature.

4. Staff meetings and curriculum meetings.

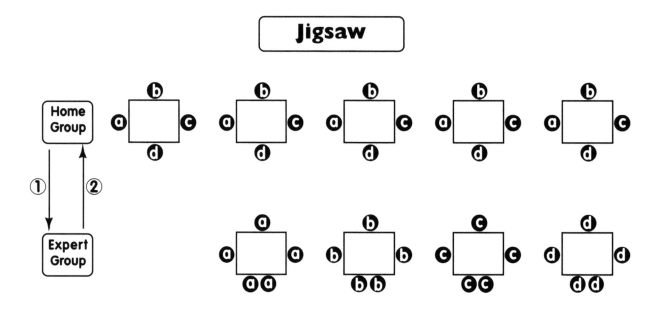

SUE 1 _____

_____

_____

_____

SUE 2 _____

_____

_____

_____

Triad

This is a useful strategy to have all students on task. A topic needs to be chosen and possibly discussed in an open forum. The reason for this is to highlight some of the basic information concerning that topic. The topic may be responsibilities and privileges experienced in a democracy and could have been the focus of a few formal lessons.

Task

Students are to share their ideas on this topic as well as offer opinions.

Process

1. Students are to group themselves in threes and designate themselves as either *A, B* or *C*.

2. *A* and *B* sit opposite each other with their knees almost touching. *A* has to speak slowly to *B*, giving his/her opinion and knowledge concerning the topic. *B* must remain attentive and maintain eye contact.

3. Meanwhile, *C*, who is sitting to the side of *A* and *B*, is recording everything said by *A*. After a minute or two, *B* may ask a question of *A* to maintain the flow of ideas. *C* records the question and subsequent answers.

4. When the conversation dries up, *A* and *B* turn to look at *C* and *C* reads from the notes. *A* may disagree with parts of the transcript or be amazed at how someone else interpreted his/her words. A short discussion then follows to clarify what was said and heard.

5. *A* now moves into the recorder's chair, *B* moves into the speaker's chair and *C* now moves into the listener's chair, and the process starts again. At the completion of this round, one more swap takes place.

Observation

- It is not always necessary to have all three rounds. However, if there are three different topics, then there will be sufficient novelty to ask all three students to play all three roles, whereas this could become tedious if the same topic is covered three times.

- I have enjoyed using this strategy, because apart from the obvious benefits of giving students time to reflect on their knowledge in a less public setting, the skill of listening and concentrating is also being employed. Good listening is possibly the basis of all learning, for without it, the reason and purpose of the lessons are often misunderstood. Honouring another person by maintaining eye contact is something else which is sadly lacking with so many of us, and as a result, a **Triad** may help in promoting this behaviour.

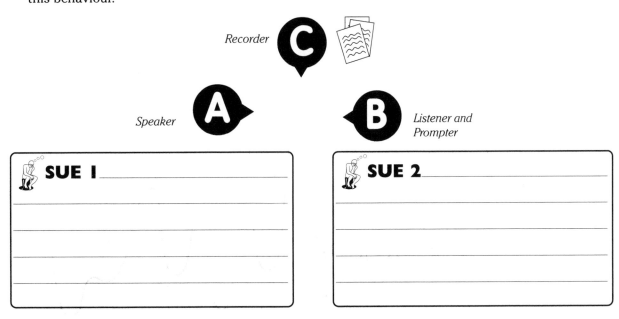

Recorder **C**

Speaker **A**   **B** Listener and Prompter

SUE 1 _____

SUE 2 _____

Doughnut or Inner-Outer Circle

This is a more personal form of brainstorming. It requires equal numbers of thinkers, so the teacher may have to fill in if the group has an odd number of students.

Process

Divide the class into two concentric circles with the inner circle facing the people in the outer circle. This is a useful strategy for developing debatable issues where the inner circle must argue in favour of point *A* while the outer circle argues in favour of point *B*. No attempt is made to take notes. Instead the thinkers need to remember what is being said. Once the conversation or discussion begins to slow down, ask the outer circle to move three places to the right, so that everyone has a new sparring partner. This process can be repeated several times. Then tell all involved to reverse their roles without moving from their positions (those in the inner circle remain there) so that those who were defending Point A, are now defending Point B and vice versa. This is a useful device in that it encourages **Other Point of View** thinking.

I particularly use this in 'The Reconciliation of Goldilocks & the Three Bears', where half the class (inner circle) is designated as Goldilocks whose task it is to ask for forgiveness of the Bears, the other half or outer circle. The negotiations run for 1-2 minutes before the rotation takes place, then another 1-2 minutes for the second attempt by Goldilocks to seek forgiveness. On the fourth rotation, I swap the roles, often with interesting results. Remember the old Indian saying "Don't judge a person until you have walked one mile in his moccasins!" **The Other Point of View** perspective is often a sobering and moderating experience. At the conclusion of the **Doughnut**, thinkers go back to their own desks or groups in order to write a summary of their findings or to compile a final report.

Reservation

Though I have found this to be an extremely useful and lively strategy involving the whole class, it is possible that a few students may find the closeness of the contact too intimidating. However, this seldom occurred and I have noticed that they have seen the strategy through.

Observation

- This is a very lively strategy which creates energy in the classroom and clearly places the onus on the learners.
- The whole strategy can last as little as 5–7 minutes and has greater value if a debriefing session takes place.

B — Outer Circle *(facing inwards)*

A

— Inner Circle *(facing outwards)*

SUE 1 _____	SUE 2 _____

Think: Pair: Share

One of the major problems in any thinking environment is the perception that speed of response is somehow linked to intelligence or ability. This may be useful for 'Sale of the Century' type shows, but can be disastrous for good thinking as it will channel and restrict thinking in several situations. I explain this to students after asking them questions such as, "Who will get married one day?" Without fail, a sea of hands goes up in a split second. Such little thought for such an important decision! I point this out and introduce the **Think: Pair: Share** (**T:P:S**) strategy as an antidote for such thinking.

Process

1. Number off the students in pairs.

2. Pose the question.

3. Students must consider the question without speaking for at least 20 seconds, generating as many answers as possible or thinking in great depth. (**Think**)

4. Students now work in pairs, taking it in turns to listen to each others' ideas and then discussing similarities and differences for one to two minutes. Students are generally asked to agree on an answer. (**Pair**)

5. Now the teacher invites some, several or all pairs to respond. (**Share**) A useful understanding to establish is for a group to say 'ditto' if a previous group has shared what they were about to say. This prevents a waste of time through repetition and encourages them to listen to other people.

Observation

- This is another type of brainstorm which ensures that all learners are on task and one which avoids some of the problems of a whole-class brainstorm. This is also similar to the **1:3:Share** or the **1:4:Share** strategy.

- Students are often anaesthetised in the area of responding to a question because of the presence of extroverts or more dominant students. The **T:P:S** negates this problem and allows the more reflective student a better chance to express ideas.

- Shyer students often welcome this strategy because they are working in a smaller group and the other person can offer the feedback if necessary.

SUE 1 _____

SUE 2 _____

1:4:Publish:Circle:Refine
(Eric Frangenheim)

This is an extremely powerful cooperative process which calls for creative thinking and critical reflection within the orbit of both interpersonal and intrapersonal intelligence.

Task

To design a mission statement on thinking in our school.

Process

In groups of four:

Step 1   Write a mission statement of your own. (**1**)

Step 2   Share your idea with the other three in your group and discuss the different products. Your task is now to create one synthesised statement. (**4**)

Step 3   Decide on one synthesised mission statement and write this clearly onto a larger piece of paper. (As an added option, you could ask the team to write down the strategy used to synthesise the four statements into one. Write this at the foot of the page. This is useful in terms of seeing how different groups cooperate.) (**Publish**)

Step 4   Post the large piece of paper on the wall and leave one member of the group behind as the 'Explainer' or 'Defender'. There will now be 7-8 such mission statements around the classroom wall, each with one 'Defender' next to that statement. The groups of three now move around the room, reading and discussing the contents of the other mission statements and possibly asking questions of the various 'Defenders'. As they do this, it is important to take notes as they progress around the room. (**Circle**) It is not necessary to visit every sheet/station, but at least four should be considered.

Step 5   Go back to your home group, discuss the notes you made and the new understandings generated from circling the room, and discuss ways to improve your mission statement. Now refine your statement and share with the whole class. (**Refine**)

Observation

I have used this strategy many times with teachers and students. I once used it to ask Year 7 students the definition of Democracy. This was soon after their return from Canberra. Once they had completed the process, they were asked to write a letter to someone in some place which had little or no democracy and try to encourage them to migrate to Australia, explaining the advantages of our democratic way of life. This was the culminating activity using the persuasive genre. It certainly seemed to work extremely well!

In terms of Human Relations Education or in any pastoral care group, topics such as bullying, the various 'isms' can be explored with a view to designing a brief mission statement, mini anthem, slogan, etc. It involves all learners and the resulting hybrid product can be extremely motivating by giving a sense of ownership to many students.

I have used this strategy several times when running workshops for trainers, facilitators and educators from government departments and private industry. They have been particularly impressed with this strategy as a means of encouraging learners to focus, clarify, listen, adapt, refine and use the power of synergy to produce a clear and effective result.

SUE 1	SUE 2

Think: Whisper: Refine: Share
(Eric Frangenheim)

This strategy encourages students to listen to other people's ideas and allows them to refine and develop their original ideas in a spirit of cooperative thinking. It also discourages satisfaction with an immediate response.

Process

1. Students need to be organised into groups of four, and designated as *A, B, C* and *D*.

2. All students then listen to the question and think of an answer to the problem. For example, the question or problem to be solved is "How could Goldilocks have avoided becoming lost in the forest?" (**Think**)

3. At a given signal, *A* whispers his solution to *B* while *C* whispers her solution to *D*. Then *B* offers her solution to *C* and *D* tells *A* his solution. In this way, each member of the group is now likely to have his or her own solution plus that of another member of the group. (**Whisper**)

4. Without any talking, students think of their first solution and the solution offered by the other person and now attempt to refine or improve their thinking in order to generate an even better idea. (**Refine**)

5. The students now share all four new ideas within the group, discuss each one and attempt to present a solution based on the discussion. Each group then presents one solution to the class. (**Share**)

Observation

*   It is useful to write the steps on the board and draw a simple diagram of the flow of whispered ideas between A, B, C and D.

*   Though this takes some time, it does encourage the useful and necessary social skills of listening and sharing.

*   It also encourages the cognitive skills of **comparing**, **understanding**, **focusing** on the problem, **analysing** in a critical manner one's own idea and that of the other person and then **synthesising** the various solutions into one proposal.

*   More importantly, it encourages the virtue of delayed gratification.

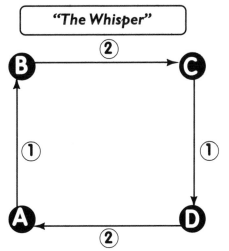

"The Whisper"

SUE 1 _____

SUE 2 _____

Pairs and RAS Alert

I had often noticed that when I showed part of a video or read a piece of text and then attempted to encourage discussion, many students had switched off and did not take part in discussions. I have since learnt about a feature of our brain known as the Reticular Activating System which is part of our fight or flight mechanism. It recognises stimuli which we have programmed into our minds. For example, if you were to go shopping for blue suede shoes, you would notice these everywhere you went, not only in shop window displays, but also on the feet of old rockers. It is the same with paranoia. If you expect sarcasm, you will imagine it everywhere, even if it is not intended.

So how do we turn this to our advantage in the classroom?

Process

The teacher need to explain each of these steps in advance of showing the video/demonstration/reading so that they have a clear idea of the big picture

Step 1. Organise students into pairs; one student is designated as A, the other as B.

Step 2. Alert the students (thus the term 'RAS Alert') to the real PURPOSE of the video/ reading/ demonstration. Be sure to use powerful language ion order to capture their attention and convince them that the following is worthy of their attention. For example, if the material is to do with some man-made disaster, it may be useful to state, "We are going to see a video where lives were needlessly lost through the sheer incompetence and unbridled ego of certain people in positions of extreme authority" instead of saying "We are going to look at a video of a train accident" (a bit bland?). Then the teacher draws up an organiser (below) on the board and asks each student to do the same with a piece of paper. The teacher clearly states, 'During the course of the video, you will notice **6 causes** of this disaster, **4 ways it could have been avoided**, **2 possible attempts to cover-up** and **3 opinions**. As the teacher states each of these 4 parts, she/he inserts this into the organiser and underlines it, asking the students to do the same. In this way, the students' RAS has been clearly alerted to the real purpose of watching this video.

6 x causes	4 x possible avoidance
• •	• •
2 x Cover-up	3 x Opinion
• •	• •

Step 3. The teacher tells the class that their memory is FANTASTIC and asks them to leave their pens on the table and observe the video.

Step 4. In each pair, Students A and B take turns listing the information being sought. Both enter the data on their respective retrieval sheet, always taking turns to offer data. If one is stuck, he/she can say 'Pass' and the other student can offer more data.

Step 5. The teacher can complete a quick 'whip around', collecting the top ideas from the students, ensuring that the major points have been noticed, adding anything they may have missed.

Observation

This strategy encourages a sense of team work, improves focus for both teacher and students, encourages listening and concentration and engages students in successful behaviours. It is also quick and engenders a sense of FUN!

Applications

Performance (Drama): Students are shown a video of an amateur play or production and complete the retrieval chart using **Pairs and RAS Alert**.

2 pieces of poor acting	3 clever pieces of improvisation	4 excellent props
• •	• •	• •

 SUE 1 _____

_____

_____

_____

 SUE 2 _____

_____

_____

_____

    Eric Frangenheim ©

Reflections from Other Classrooms

I have invited several teachers and consultants to contribute their reflections on the use of specific thinking tools in their classrooms or workshops. All these teachers/consultants are enthusiastic promoters of thinking in learning environments and realise the value of the explicit use of appropriate tools. I hope you enjoy their insights and reflections of their own practice and that this will both affirm and inspire you in what you do.

Straw Polling

Laurie Kelly

All the theory on learning says that it is important to recognise prior knowledge of the learner or at least get the learner to reflect on their own thinking about the topic before seeking to introduce new ideas. Traditionally this has been done by giving a question to the whole class and seeking a response. Hands may or may not go up with various levels of enthusiasm and one person is asked to give 'the' answer. This strategy really only tells the instructor what that one person knows and not the knowledge within the group.

There are other strategies that can be used to give the instructor some understanding of the group's existing knowledge which are fun, non threatening and involve the four perceptual models of Visual, Auditory, Kinesethics and Tactile. They can also be used for group discussion, decision making and feedback.

THREE IDEAS

A. Coloured Cards

Process

Here you offer each group member three cards.

RED CARD   is held up if you *disagree* with the question being asked

YELLOW CARD is held up if you are *unsure*

GREEN CARD   is held up if you *agree*

Observation

This can produce a lot of fun, build inquisitiveness and a lot of discussion. It most importantly allows the instructor to see immediately the knowledge of the whole group.

B. Traffic Signs

Process

This is similar except that the three cards are all white but have traffic lights circled with the top circle on one card coloured red for disagreement, the middle circle of another card coloured yellow for unsure and the bottom circle of the third card coloured green to represent agreement

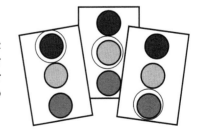

Observation

The advantage of this method of straw polling is that the group show their decision to the instructor and only he/she can see at a quick glance where the group's thinking is. This can save embarrassment to those who do not know the 'right' answer.

C. Human Print Out

This can be used to have the group take a position on a particular issue and again allow the instructor to quickly assess the group's level of understanding and readiness for further challenge.

Process

Have three or five witches hats or chairs around the room to represent various levels of agreement or disagreement to the stated position.

Participants get up from their chairs and move to the position which feels comfortable for them.

Observation

This exercise can generate physical energy in the room, debate and discussion as well as allowing the instructor and group to see the diversity of thinking in the room.

General Observations

These three simple techniques can assist the instructor to assess the knowledge in the room as well as act as a stimulus for generating interest and allowing individuals to see the diversity of thinking.

All three methods can be used after group discussion when the group as a whole have to agree on the coloured card traffic light or position where the group will stand.

About Laurie Kelly

Director of Mindworks Australia Pty Ltd

Laurie holds a Bachelor of Education and is a qualified Educational Kinesiologist. He has been opening up the mysteries of the mind to audiences from all walks of life for over 14 years.

Mindworks, a management consultancy business based in Brisbane with clients around Australia, was founded by Laurie in 1986. It is an organisation helping people understand how their minds work and how this understanding can lead to a better appreciation of how and why they behave in certain ways.

Phone: 71 7 3289 4977
email: mindworks@pacific.net.au
Info@mindworksteam.com.au
www.mindworksteam.com.au

Particularly for Science Teaching

John Hunt

P.O.E. (Predict, Observe, Explain)

This can be varied as a P.R.O.E. (Predict, Reason, Observe, Explain): a classic strategy that appears to be made for science investigations. This format can be used to present a report from an investigation combining illustrations, annotations and more traditional written forms of communication.

Predict: what do I think is going to happen?

Reason: why do I think this is going to happen?

Observe: what did I observe happen during the investigation?

Explain: why do I think this happened?

This strategy is both a developmental (or formative) record of learning and a summative work sample at the conclusion of a project or investigation. It is not necessary to use a grid format. The headings alone could be used.

Predict	Reason	Observe	Explain
What might happen when I place a marble into containers of different liquids? eg honey, vinegar, sewing machine oil, cooking oil, water, lemonade.	For each prediction, ask the learners to give a simple explanation. Annotated diagrams might be used as well.	What did the learner observe? Was this in conflict with their prediction? How did they manage this conflict if present?	This is the point at which the teacher explores the possible conflict and needs to listen to the many conversations. How close are the learners to understanding the concept being investigated?

POE Examples

Lower Primary	Middle Primary	Upper Primary
Provide learners with a selection of objects from around the home or classroom. Familiarity is good! Ask learners to predict which will float. Make a record of these predictions. Ask learners to provide their reason/s for making their predictions. Observe and record results of investigations to test the predictions. Can learners explain any observations, particularly the anomalies?	Make available a collection of familiar objects. Ask learners to predict which will be attracted to a magnet. Ask learners to provide their reason/s for making their predictions. Test these predictions and observe what happens. Keep a record. Ask learners to explain what is observed, particularly any anomalies.	Establish a collection of solid objects that are familiar to the learners. Some should conduct an electric current while others will not. Ask learners to predict which will allow a current to flow in a simple circuit. Ask learners to provide their reason/s for making their predictions. Test these predictions and observe what happens. Record observations. At this level, learners should be using words such as conductors and insulators to explain their observations.

K.W.H.L

John Hunt

This is the acronym for (what do I already **Know**? **What** do I need to know? **How** I will find out? and what did I **Learn**?) – a variation on a KWL, this strategy places an emphasis on considering the many resources that are available as the learner seeks an answer. A matrix of this type enables the teacher to support the learner/s during the inquiry phases of a project, point to appropriate resources and build a work sample that indicates what has been learned.

It is not necessary to use the grid format presented here. The use of a grid imposes artificial and confusing boundaries for learners who may have more or less to add to a heading.

what do I **K**now?	**W**hat do I want to know?	**H**ow will I find out?	what did I **L**earn?
This is a fundamental component of the 'constructivist classroom' – what do my learners know? Concept mapping or brainstorming can establish 'what is known'.	Allowing learners to manage their learning ensures a better match to learner interests and a greater chance of achieving enhanced outcomes. When learners are actively involved in the decision-making, better learning occurs.	Rather than relying on research from books, learners will welcome the opportunity to explore CDs, interrogate databases and the Internet and speak with guests. This caters for the many learning styles in the classroom and ensures learners are engaged with current information and trends.	What did the learner gain from this experience? What conceptual understanding is evident? This might be elicited through revisiting a previously completed concept map or through group brainstorming.

KWHL Examples

Lower Primary	Middle Primary	Upper Primary
What do learners know about things that float and things that sink? *– brainstorming, simple mapping, annotated diagrams, discussions* What do they want to know about floating and sinking? *– what does the curriculum tell me?* What investigations can help develop an understanding? What resources will provide an explanation? How will I know what has been learned? *– brainstorming, simple mapping, annotated diagrams, multiple intelligence presentation, models, pictures*	What do learners know about rainforest animals and the relationship between animals of the rainforest? *– brainstorming, simple mapping* What do they want to know? *– discussion resulting from brainstorming* What will be available and useful? What are the resources I can find? Are there any human resources (experts)? How will I know what the learner has learned? *– brainstorming, simple mapping, models made, pictures drawn*	What do my learners know about simple electric circuits? *– brainstorming, simple mapping, annotated diagrams, multiple intelligence presentation, drama, music* What do they want to know about simple circuits? *– what does the curriculum tell me?* What investigations can help develop an understanding? What resources will provide an explanation? Are there any human resources (experts)? How will I know what has been learned? *– brainstorming, simple mapping, annotated diagrams, multiple intelligence presentation, models, pictures*

Concept Mapping
John Hunt

This is not to be confused with spider maps and thinking maps and has strong links to the KWHL previously mentioned. Concept maps can be used to provide the Know and Learn elements. Concept maps reduce the writing and text demands for learners; after all, are we assessing writing skills of science concepts? *'Concept maps are based on constructivist principles and assume that people have mental images of the ways their ideas fit together'*, (Harrison, 1999 Volume 2 Issue 4 The Queensland Science Teacher). They have a basis in Ausubel's theory of 'meaningful learning' and owe much to the work of Joseph Novak (http://www2.ucsc.edu/mlrg/).

Learners do not intuitively work well with concept maps, although once they have developed a familiarity with them, you will be surprised at the ease with which they work with and use them. Scaffolding their use is the best way to promote them as a means of communication and as a review and/or assessment device.

Concept maps make explicit the links between cells of the map. They explain the connection/s between ideas.

For example:

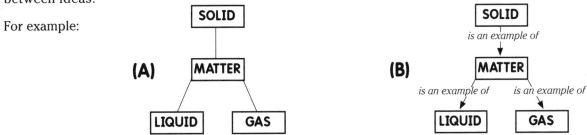

Example A above is a thinking map, whilst **Example B** is moving towards a concept map and contains the 'big concept' (MATTER) and the first subordinate (or level) of information. It also contains ideas making clearer the links between the concepts.

In a concept map, the connecting expressions are important as they indicate how the learner makes the conceptual link to the main concept, idea or proposition.

If Example B was to be continued and the reason for the links established, then it is an example of a concept map demonstrating a higher level of understanding. An example of such a map can be found **below.**

Can you add more levels of ideas to this concept map?

Remember, add the reason for the link to each pair of ideas.

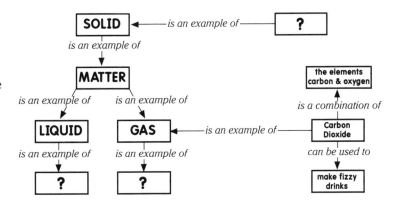

On the concept map above, note that the direction of the arrow indicates the sentence-like structure of the link between the ideas eg. [Carbon dioxide] is an example of a [gas].

Concept maps such as this provide a degree of scaffolding, showing learners how to complete them. If this map had been completed in more detail, it would show some of the ideas held by learners at the beginning of a unit of work – the **KNOW**. If it is handed back to students at completion of study, they should be allowed to make alterations and additions to it, showing the **LEARN**. Likewise, you might encourage your learners to modify their maps as the unit progresses – the point in time moments when new ideas and understandings occur. Being able to modify maps as learning occurs shows the learner that assessment does not have to be the final element of an unit of work.

Concept Map Examples

Lower Primary

In the early years of schooling, concept mapping is best developed drawing from familiar situations, for example, how to make 'gloop'

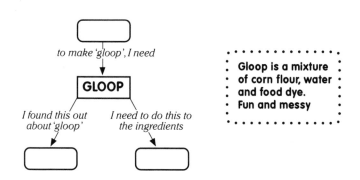

Middle Primary

In the Middle Years, provide learners with an envelope containing words associated with either 'water cycle', food chains/food webs or magnets. These ideas and concepts might be developed through a brainstorming session.

Ask learners to use these words (and others they may know about) to construct a concept map indicating the link between the ideas. Provide spare paper for learners to add their own words.

Upper Primary

Provide learners with a partially completed concept map and a list of words that could be used to complete it. This could be built from the words learners suggest during a group brainstorming session.

The 'big idea' for this concept is **ELECTRICITY**.

For example, in the case of electricity, a word list might include: battery, bulb, wires, terminal, positive, negative, simple circuit, conductors, insulators, copper, metal, plastic, aluminium, motor, magnetism, magnet,

The information gained by the teacher when this map is first completed provides a good indication of the experiences needed to build a more complex conceptual understanding for the learner.

About John Hunt

John Hunt lectures in Science, Technology and ICTs for learning at Central Queensland University (Bundaberg). He was formerly Senior Training Officer at AccessED and has worked in the area of primary science and technology for 20 years. His research interests include mentoring in primary science, impediments to the implementation of science and technology curricula and innovation in the use of ICTs to deliver learning outcomes.

Telephone: 71 7 4150 7111
Fax: 71 7 4150 7030
Email: j.hunt@cqu.edu.au

The Architecture Of Thinking:
Buttresses, Frameworks, Scaffolds And Other
Inspirational Ways Of Supporting Thinking
(or how to carry an analogy too far!)
Margaret Bishop (Bishop PD)

Seeing someone come to the REALISATION that they have the CAPACITY to THINK their very own thoughts, to RESPOND concisely and effectively to a challenging question or to be able to CONTRIBUTE their ORIGINAL PERCEPTIONS to a discussion, has to be one of the most rewarding moments of teaching – any sort of teaching. Often referred to as the AHA moment, this occurs when an individual has an insight into just what they are capable of when given the opportunity to scaffold their thinking. I am privileged to witness many of these great moments as I work with teachers and students across Australia and share the joy of discovery and the growth in learning that follows.

Questioning Thinking

Thinking clearly, critically, rationally, laterally, divergently or creatively is expected of all of us at some time in our daily lives, both at work and leisure. Most of us 'have-a-go' and bumble along, relying on the fact that no one's likely to examine us too closely on the outcomes. But then there are those times when some 'smart alec' will pose one of those truly challenging (or terrifying) questions: "How did that (idea, thought) get inside your head?" (primary students love to ponder that one) or '"What basis do you have for making that assumption/response?" (an all-age challenger if ever there was one!) and of course we must not forget that beauty: "How did you arrive at that conclusion?" (requiring a blow-by-blow description of the thought processes involved – the deliberations, machinations and manoeuvrings of a magnificent (muddled?) mind!)

So, I got to thinking about (and observing more keenly) how students and teachers handled this 'thinking' thing. In classrooms and workshop venues across Australia I have the opportunity of working with thinkers, young and not so young, who are contributing to the shaping of all our futures. The most successful of these seem to be able to move freely between the roles of teacher and learner. Whether they are in 'teacher' or 'learner' role, they seek out better ways of scaffolding and framing their thinking processes.

This active approach was very much evident when I worked with a group of Year 10 students who had been asked to 'discuss' a number of newspaper and journal articles about *cloning*. Most students seemed willing to 'have-a-go' and the 'buzz' of discussion soon filled the room. Within a few minutes however, I noticed some groups seemed to have 'dried up' while others seemed at a loss as to where this 'discussion' should take them and were looking to the teacher for more instructions or were simply losing focus altogether. What they needed was some way of framing the discussion that would help guide them towards the desired outcome. As teachers we are (usually) pretty clear in our own minds (and plans) about what exactly we expect our students to get out of a discussion or examination of particular resources. However, we often fail to be *explicit* in our directions to students leaving them to stumble around in the dark, unsure of what it is they are looking for – like sending them on a journey without knowing the destination.

Icon Prompt
Margaret Bishop (Bishop PD)

Well, it's moments like this that a good thinking strategy never goes astray! It was time to introduce a discussion focus tool – the ICON PROMPT. Over many years, I'd noticed that most topics for discussion (in fact most issues in life) seem to revolve around a few key elements: "Who stood to gain (was happy)?" "Who stood to lose (was sad)?" "What part did money play?" and, "What other questions/issues were raised or left unanswered?" By linking these questions to a universally recognised icon or symbol, a simple strategy to scaffold discussions was born!

The Icon Prompt activity sheets were handed out and explained and the Year 10's once again set about the business of discussing *'cloning'*. It quickly became apparent that the students were engaged in a way they hadn't been earlier. They now had something they could get their teeth into – they could focus more clearly on the task and study the articles with particular questions in mind. Like scaffolding on buildings, the Icon Prompt provided sound support at the foundation levels of thinking (knowledge and understanding) while at the same time encouraging the students to reflect on issues that were inherent to the discussion but not necessarily obvious thus shifting them to higher-order thinking.

Although in this case, the Icon Prompt was used to orientate the students to the topic, I have also successfully used this strategy at the end of a unit of work to re-focus the discussion. By comparing their original Icon Prompt notes with those completed after they have researched the topic, students will have tangible evidence of how their thinking and learning has expanded. I am a great believer that all ideas should be open to improvement and to this end I challenge students and teachers to explore other icons that are universally understood and that could add another dimension to discussion topics e.g. the heart icon ❤ could provide the Intrapersonal learner (and others) with an opportunity to comment on their personal response/feelings about a particular issue.

ICON PROMPT©

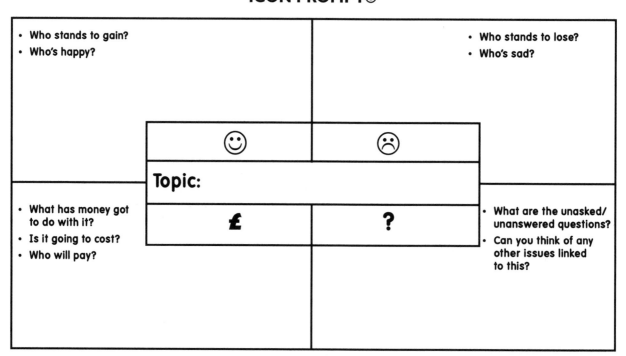

Picture Strategy 'With a Twist'!
Margaret Bishop (Bishop PD)

Never one to let go of a good thing, I've recorded some 'brilliant' results from using Picture Strategy 'with a twist!' For those of you unfamiliar with this particular strategy, I'll give you a quick rundown and then explain the 'twist'! [You can also check out Picture Strategy (by Tony Ryan) on the Xpata Lesson Planner on www.xpata.com – go to the Activity Development Page and it's listed under Cognitive Strategies.] Any Picture can be used as stimuli for a brainstorming session to generate ideas that can later be filtered to focus on a particular outcome. By using a picture or drawing that is abstract and therefore open to interpretation, there's a better chance of generating more creative responses. Teachers often tell me that they either missed out on creative juices or that they've dried up from leaving the lid off!! Well, to test this view, I thought I'd introduce a group of teachers in Perth to a good dose of Thinking Strategies and then watch what happened. Talk about creative!

Process

Step 1. I asked the teachers (primary and secondary) to look at a 'Picture' of randomly placed circles that I had drawn on the whiteboard (see illustration) and asked them to consider what the circles or shape reminded them of.

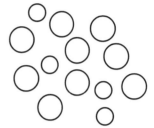

Step 2. Each group then appointed a recorder to write down all the ideas that were generated e.g. bubbles, rain, fabric and so on. We then use the co-operative strategy **Round Robin** to pass these recording sheets on to the next group for them to peruse and add new ideas. The sheets continued to be passed from group to group with the same instructions – *Read the list first and then add something that you've not already recorded on a previous sheet.*

Step 3. Now for the '*twist*' as promised! As the ideas accumulated, I applied a *filter* e.g. Each group was asked to think of mathematical associations for the shapes (or science, interesting words (language), history, geography and so on depending on the outcome in mind). These new ideas were added to the list and the groups then sorted and labelled the ideas written previously e.g. 'M' for maths ideas, 'SC' for science.

(In this workshop, as I was working with teachers who taught across a wide range of ages and content areas, I continued the Round Robin and applied a new filter at each change so that the lists of ideas they'd generated, had several 'sortings'. If you're working with a class of students in one subject area, you could apply more specific filters e.g. think of (or look for) things in the room, in the school grounds, on the bus to school/home, things in the atmosphere or on the ground etc but only *after* they've generated their own ideas from viewing the stimulus 'Picture'.)

Step 4. I then asked each group to focus on a particular aspect of the 'sorting' e.g. science, mathematics, language (lovely words!) and so on. They had to use the list of ideas on their sheet to 'teach' the rest of the class 'something' in the subject area I'd allocated to them. One group was asked to use the ideas to 'educate' the rest of us about any current issue that affected many countries. Another group was given the task of writing a rap or song incorporating as many of the interesting words that were on their particular list. (I sometimes ask students to write a haiku, a poem or a story instead of a rap and I often add a filter e.g. Write a haiku using some of the words on your list to explain what steam is!) Yet another group were to teach the rest of us some basic concept in science. Each group was also asked to incorporate visual, oral, physical, musical elements or a combination of these in their presentation to the whole group.

Reflection

So, back to the question of teachers' creativity or lack of it. If the posters, raps, mimes, songs and charts presented by this group are any indication, then creativity is certainly alive and growing in the teaching profession. Everyone was thrilled with their efforts and couldn't quite believe that all this wonderful, nay, brilliant work could have been generated by a simple drawing of a few circles!

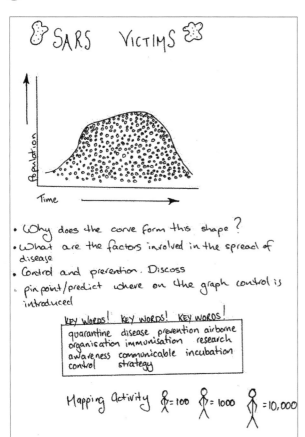

Poster 1: SARS VICTIMS

Poster 2: CHAMPAGNE POPS

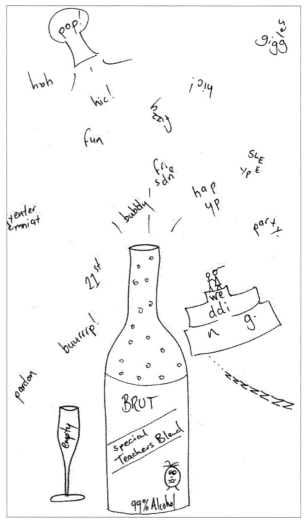

Poster 3: THE LOTTO LIFE

The Human Continuum
Margaret Bishop (Bishop PD)

Now I certainly can't finish off my allotted space without sharing what I consider to be one of the most versatile co-operative/cognitive strategies that I've used – the **Human Continuum**. As this strategy involves physical activity it appeals to the Body/Kinaesthetic learner by getting them up and moving. If it is being used to focus thinking on a particular 'issue' e.g. Capital Punishment in Australia, then it has the added appeal of having the participants literally 'taking a stand' to indicate their point of view on the topic in question. I've used Human Continuum with all ages, from preschoolers to really old teachers (!) e.g. recalling the steps in a Pancake recipe with a bunch of not-yet-reading Year 1's (we drew each step on a card and then the children arranged themselves in order from start to finish); sequencing the different 'pages' and processes involved in a new software program at secondary level. (I placed Post-It Notes on each student's computer asking a specific question e.g. "Where in the program is the Activity Development Page?" or "What does the term 'Save to File' mean" and "Where is that function used?" Some Post-Its also referred to new or unfamiliar technical terms that were used in the software. The students had to find the information by examining the software program in a given time frame and then position themselves on the Human Continuum according to where the function occurred between loading the program and closing it down); and of course as a focussing strategy like debating the pros and cons of Capital Punishment with teachers and pre-service trainees. (I started off with a broad question – Do you agree/strongly agree or disagree/strongly disagree with Capital Punishment? Once everyone had placed himself or herself along the continuum, I continued to add a little more information, gradually narrowing the parameters of the issue by personalising the circumstances. Everyone soon realised that it was much easier to have an opinion in a 'vacuum'!)

Topic: *Capital Punishment in Australia*

Step 1. Create sufficient space in the room for all participants to form a line (curved or straight).

Step 2. Make a statement e.g. Australia should introduce Capital Punishment!

Step 3. Participants who strongly **agree** with the statement should move to the left end of the line (appropriate signs or symbols could be placed at either end of the continuum – **Agree**/**Disagree**, + -). Those who **disagree** move to the right end of the line to indicate the strength of their belief in the statement.

Step 4. Question the participants briefly about their reasons for taking up the position they have chosen.

Step 5. Begin to focus the issue by providing additional information or by narrowing the parameters of the original statement e.g. "*The crime in question is the most heinous that can be committed.*" Participants move again to reflect their changing views. (If time permits check why some people changed positions and others not.)

Step 6. Play devil's advocate by continuing to focus the issue by introducing more explicit detail that may personalise the argument for some participants. e.g. "*The victim of the crime was a child.*" Participants move or stay in position according to their response to new circumstances. Continue narrowing the parameters and perhaps introduce a surprise final element!

When I am working with adults or senior students I can be more explicit about the information given as there are any number of reports of such crimes, the particulars of which can be generalised:

- "*The crime was committed in your town/suburb/street.*"
- "*The victim is known to you – within your inner circle – school, work, friend of friend etc.*"
- "*The victim is a member of your own family.*"
- "*The government has decided that the execution is to be carried out by a supporter of Capital Punishment who will be selected by ballot.*"
- "*The government has also decreed that the manner of execution is to mirror the crime – literally an eye for an eye!*"
- "*The victim, in the case in question, was garrotted/stabbed/bashed with a hammer etc.*"

And now for the final twist!

- *"The perpetrator is also a member of your family!"*
- Note that after each successive new detail, participants are asked to reposition themselves and explain their stance to a person next to them.

Applications: Forming opinions

Analysing point of view

Sequencing series of events – Human Timeline

Sequencing steps in a process e.g. recipe, computer program

Value Add by: a] After students have researched and broadened their understanding of the topic, ask them to reform the Human Continuum. Have they changed their Point of View/ position? Why?

b] Give students cards that illustrate an event, a step in a process, or a part of a whole and ask them to take up a position in line according to where their event, step or part would be placed in relation to the cards the other students are holding.

About Margaret Bishop

Margaret Bishop is a 'peripatetic' teacher as well as director of Bishop Education (Resources and Services) and Bishop PD. She is the chief trainer for the Xpata Lesson Planner and is accredited to Rodin Educational Consultancy. As part of the dynamic trio, 'The Three Wise Women', with Anne Baker and Beth Wood, she is involved in the ongoing development of strategies for scaffolding thinking that can be utilised by anyone, from grandmothers to 'grand' managers!

Margaret believes that the goal of teaching at all levels is to transfer 'ownership of learning'. As a presenter and consultant, both in Australia and overseas, Margaret focuses on the importance of understanding and making explicit the teaching/learning connection. Margaret is a committed 'learning revolutionary' who aims to support life-long learning by modelling productive thinking and learning strategies.

Email: bisghoped@bigpond.com

Outlining Outcomes for Use in the Classroom
Kathleen Layton

1. Introduction

Among the avalanche of recent educational innovations that have been touted as the panacea for providing students with the coping skills required in our fast-changing world, the pedagogical 'saviour' I have found to deliver is 'outcomes-based teaching and learning'.

Stated simply, outcomes-based teaching and learning is about determining, in advance, the outcomes that *will* be achieved through the teaching and learning interaction, rather than hoping that desirable objectives will result by default. It involves planning a programme that *will* achieve the predetermined outcomes, implementing that programme and assessing the standards reached in achieving the chosen outcomes.

2. Using a Planning Model

It is vital to have a planning framework for an outcomes curriculum unit. It allows the teacher to:

(a) define the theme or concept that will house the outcomes

(b) select, decode and unpack appropriate outcomes

(c) select outcomes that will be assessed and then plan upfront assessment of these outcomes

(d) identify a variety of teaching and learning tasks for the implementation of each outcome.

Using a planning model format gives the teacher a step-by-step guide covering every implementation step from theme choice through to reporting.

Should teachers plan every detail of the unit?

Yes they should to begin with. Also there are some outcomes that will always need to be unpacked by the teacher beforehand. However, when students gain confidence with outcome units, it is great to allow their involvement in the decoding unpacking and assessment ideas for their outcomes as this practice gives students ownership of their learning. Students can see what they have to know (content) and what they have to do (process verb) and start to brainstorm how they are going to demonstrate these outcomes.

I find student involvement leads to open discussion of the outcomes material and can help students clarify the content and process (verb) of each outcome. I have found also that students' involvement in the assessment decision-making motivates them to generate new ideas and suggestions for the assessment demonstration.

3. The Nuts and Bolts of Planning

The key to planning is the decoding and unpacking of each outcome and the anticipated evidence that will demonstrate that an outcome has been achieved. The latter are commonly called **standards or indicators**.

For the purpose of this chapter I shall select an end-of-unit project outcome and show how to decode and unpack it. Then I shall display the assessment standards that were used to assess the outcome. It is important to be aware that some outcomes can be assessed as homework tasks or in-class oral or written tests. Not all outcomes lend themselves to end-of-unit project tasks

4. Decoding and Unpacking an Outcome

Sample Outcome: *This S.O.S.E. outcome was used in a Year 7 Multicultural unit and was chosen so students could identify migrant groups that had contributed to Australian (cultural, economic, sporting, medical etc) history.*

TCC 4.3 *Students share empathetic responses to contributions that diverse individuals and groups have made to Australian or global history.*

4 (a) Decoding the outcome:

What does TCC 4.3 all mean?

Outcome Code: TCC = **Time, Continuity and Change** is one of four Strands from the Study of Society and the Environment (SOSE), one of the Queensland Studies Authority (QSA) eight key learning areas.

Outcome Level: 4 is one of the six sequential learning levels, in this case the students were in Year 7 (aged 12).

SOSE processes identify with the following decimal points: .1 = investigating, .2 = creating, .3 = participating, .4 = communicating and .5 = reflecting.

4 (b) Unpacking the outcome statement

TCC 4.3 *Students share empathetic responses to contributions that diverse individuals and groups have made to Australian or global history*

What students need to KNOW	What students can DO	What students need to SHOW
Read statement and circle or underline all the key words in colour eg using blue for the content words, such as nouns and adjectives *empathetic responses* *contributions* *diverse individuals/groups* *Australian history*	Select the **Do** (**verb**) words from the statement, using colour red. *share* *have made*	Brainstorm how they, the students, may show empathy for a migrant group who have contributed to a part of Australian history

Teaching and Learning Strategies	Teaching and Learning Strategies	Show Project
1 Class use dictionaries to define the above terms. Display results on a **Mind Map** 2 Brainstorm and research appropriate migrant groups, and their contributions – **display list** eg migrants workers on Snowy Mountain Scheme 3 Use a **Venn design** to contrast and compare *empathy* and *sympathy* 4 **Brainstorm creative responses** – *eg.* I could role play contributions made by Asian restaurateurs	I use generic tasks for the learning /understanding outcome verbs, including: 1 Define the verbs using **Dictionary, thesaurus, spelling** tasks 2 **Sentence making and dictation** tasks for all verbs 3 **Role play** – *students show the concept of sharing through role play* **Cross Curricula tasks**: use percentages to share in maths, share ideas and equipment in science experiment, share friendship in class activities	The class groups tended to select migrant groups represented in their own classroom. For example (a) A **debate** titled *Migrants' contributions are taken for granted* (b) A **mural** expressing empathy for the Italian migrants from cane cutters to food retailers (c) **oral presentation** describing the contributions of migrant doctors and scientists

5. Continuum from Outcome to Anticipated Evidence

Standards are the anticipated evidence of how an outcome will be demonstrated. There is a direct continuum linking the outcome to its task '*envelope*' to the *knows* and *dos* of the task to the evidence of achievement of the outcome:

Outcome	The *goal* towards which students are progressing
↓	
Task	The *envelope* used to achieve the outcomes
Know **Do**	The *outputs* of the learning task
Anticipated Evidence – the standards	The *expected* indicators of high achievement

Standards used to assess this outcome

The student can:

1   Clearly identify a migrant group
2   Clearly identify the contributions their migrant group has made to some part of Australian history
3   Identify correctly what was meant by a part of Australian history
4   Participate in the student group effectively by fulfilling his/her assigned role
5   Identify and share correctly the contributions of their migrant group
6   Use a suitable demonstrative tool for the sharing
7   Correctly respond empathetically to the stated contributions made by their migrant group
8   Choose an appropriate tool to demonstrate the outcome

This chapter is taken from a soon to be released book provisionally titled **The Outcomes Classroom**. *For details, consult the* **Austed Consulting Group** *web site: www.austed.org*

Sample Outcomes (TCC 4.3) and the term 'anticipated evidence' are taken from the Queensland Studies Authority (QSA).

For more information, talk to Kathleen Layton (Curriculum Developer)

Austed Consulting Group
PO Box 857 Cooroy Qld 4563
Phone: 71 7 5447 9128
Fax: 71 7 5447 9261
Email: austed@bigpond.com
Website www.austed.org

Austed offers the following services:

Working with Outcomes: a Show and Do workshop that allows teachers to use a tried and tested planning model that allows for easy planning and offers a wide range of strategies for implementation of classroom outcomes.

The Brainworks: a stimulating and fun-filled unit that introduces students to the workings of their brains while demonstrating how to harness brainpower for learning.

Deceptively Simple: the Power of Thinking Frameworks

Katherine Mian

In a quiet classroom somewhere in the dry tropics of central northern Queensland, a group of year elevens in an English class is busily working on shaping their interpretation of the Australian Identity. Already they have been immersed in a range of visual, aural and written text as they explore the ways in which Australians identify themselves and how film makers, writers and others shape this identity and the perceptions of both Australians and those in other countries. They have already completed a Y chart to explore their own thinking, feeling and visual perceptions of the Australian Identity.

Following this immersion, students use a PMI coupled with a CAF as thinking tools enabling them to clarify their thinking and to map their thoughts. It also provides some drama for them as they argue interpretation of the images with which they have been presented and whether or not they consider the interpretation to have positive or negative connotations for them and for others. They use the metalanguage of critical literacy to shape the vocalisation across the classroom. Sounds noisy, doesn't it but it is the noise of the gears of the mind working in overdrive. The usefulness of a teaching and learning strategy as deceptively as simple as a PMI in a senior secondary school classroom is seen in the thinking that emerges from the afternoon debate. There are opportunities for interaction as well as quiet reflection within the structure of the lesson.

My current senior English class has remnants of a group with whom I embarked on a wonderful learning journey with when they were in year nine. As soon as the thinking frameworks went up this year, there was an excited but quiet "Yessss". The students remembered the power of these thinking frameworks and that, in itself, speaks highly of them.

Students, even at the tail end of their secondary schooling are still developing their thinking processes. A PMI offers structure to the thinking process and prevents what I term 'a magical mystery tour' when students are confronted by information but do not have the means for processing it and are unaware of the intended destination of their learning.

The PMI encourages the 'inking of the thinking' on an individual or group basis allowing students to place their assumptions within a framework devoid of value judgements of the appropriateness of their analysis or evaluation of a concept. Within my classroom I work on a 1:2:4 or think, pair share to allow students an opportunity to reflect upon and value their own learnings before moving into a pair and then group situation. There are students within each classroom who enjoy an opportunity to employ their intra-personal intelligence and if I am genuine about valuing diversity in the classroom, I must provide an opportunity for each student to operate in their preferred mode. Combining 1:2:4 with any other strategy allows each to follow their learning paths.

Who's doing the thinking in this classroom? Who's learning the value of having tools to frame the higher-order thinking that is required within a senior secondary classroom?

At this point students are able to critique the mind map that a PMI provides by using the CAF (Consider All Factors) and begin to justify choices through the location of evidence or clarification of the values, attitudes and beliefs that contributed to their positioning as a response to the visual or written texts in which they have been immersed. The CAF encourages and allows for a deeper digging and moves a student beyond scratching the surface and operating at the lower levels of the thinking hierarchy, although it is important to note the value of the lower end of the scale of higher-order thinking and to state, most categorically that the students have already developed knowledge and understanding of the metalanguage of critical literacy through a Silent Card Shuffle and a KWL.

Teachers at Sarina State High School in the English Department have enriched their classroom practice by using a repertoire of teaching and learning strategies that encourage higher-order thinking and move students beyond operating at the knowledge and understanding levels. Our working environment exhibits a 1:2:4 approach.

About Katherine Mian

Head of Department (English) Sarina State High School, Queensland, Aust.

Having worked within Education Queensland for thirty three years both as a classroom teacher and an education adviser in Effective Learning and Teaching I understand the power of teaching students the 'hows' of thinking not just the 'doing of thinking'. By doing this we, as teachers, empower our students and, I believe create, what Joan Dalton would call, a future that we really want to share in. Using these thinking scaffolds in the classroom is an investment in the future. Our students will be the leaders of the future and I want them to go out into the world armed with thinking skills that allows them to **Consider All Factors**; explore both the **Plus** and **Minus** sides of all situations and to identify through this the **Interesting** things that come to the surface through this process. I want our future leaders to be able to employ thinking skills to problem solve and make decisions. I want them to identify what they already know about an issue or concept, to consider what they want to know or need to know about it and then to reflect on their learning throughout the process. Isn't this what we all want?

Lesson Plan
for Island Survival

This is the plan for an all day lesson (in fact, it takes longer than that!) which I designed for the final two years of primary school, in order to demonstrate the use of a variety of the thinking tools referred in this book to both students and a large group of teachers. I have used this in conjunction with a power point presentation which you can download from my web site (www.rodineducation.com.au and then go to Lesson Plans and Island Survival)

Outcomes

- Use of Six Thinking Hats
- Imagination and creative writing
- Team work and problem solving
- Use of specific cognitive and cooperative thinking tools
- Chronicling of ideas and progress
- Self and peer-assessment and refinement

Organisation

1. Four teams of six students. Teams of 4 to be organised by teacher

2. Each team will produce a 'Survival Journal' of all deliberations, plans, decision making and creative writing

Activity 1: Understanding the Six Thinking Hats

 1. Teacher (**T**) Input and Handout

2. Practise the Hats using the topic of 'School Holidays' – 90 secs per hat plus feedback to check for understanding.

Activity 2: Setting the Scene for the Island Survival

 T input – location near the islands of Aruba, Bonaire and Curacao off Venezuela – Students to find this location on a map – anyway they can. Web search or encyclopaedia or atlas.

Activity 3: Survival Gear – Setting more of the scene

Refugee ship of 12 and 13 year olds being sent to Florida during WW2. German torpedo attack. The captain, who is dying, tells children to abandon ship and enter lifeboats!!!! 5 minutes to collect anything that will help with survival. Captain explains that there are many islands in the area and that there is a good chance of arriving on an island within 1-2 days of being in a life boat. "What is it that you can collect from the ship and put in the life boat?" You may not say 'food' or 'medicines' as this is too general. Be specific. You have to be able to carry these items into the lifeboats which are waiting in the water next to the sinking ship.

 a) **Silent Round Robin** on A4 sheets within each group. 4 or 5 rotations.

b) Now choose only 15 items to take on your life boat. Negotiate in your teams for the final 15 items using **Yellow** and **Black Hat** statements with each item.

c) Now decide on your most valuable survival resource and plan how you will protect it.

 Use the **Tournament Prioritiser** strategy. In each team, conduct the prioritiser in groups of not more than 2 students and then negotiate on the final outcome. Report back to the whole class.

Extra Consideration

There are 4 lifeboats with basic equipment.

Use this information when planning other activities once on the island. Some teams may forget about these resources.

Bonus: Once on your life boat, each team discovers that they have other resources which can help them in their quest for survival. Teacher hands a card to each team showing their resources. Other teams do not know what they have. Note that there are two groups of students for each life boat.

Life Boat 1	Life Boat 2	Life Boat 3	Life Boat 4
• 2 oars • 1 sail • 1 small mast • 20 litre water container (empty) • 1 axe	• 2 oars • 1 bucket • 1 box with 400 malaria pills • 1 spade • 27 wire coat hangers	• 2 oars • 4 flares • 1 small packet of matches • 1 large hook with 20 metres of rope • 1 machete	• 1 oar • 1 used parachute • 1 golf bag with full set of clubs • 20 litre water container with water • 1 machete

Activity 4: Creative Writing: The Journey

Write a half page account of what happened in the 36 hour journey in the life boat, up to and including your arrival on the island.

 Y Chart

Teacher to lead students through a visualisation process starting with 'Abandon Ship', 'journey in the life boats' and 'the landing'. Each group to have 3 x A3

Y Charts, one for each phase of 'The Journey'. Teacher to start each phase with comments from the whole class, then allow 3-4 minutes for students to develop their **Y Charts**, before moving on to the next phase. At end of the 3 **Y Charts**, give students 5-8 minutes to describe their voyage. Encourage use of powerful adverbs and adjectives in order to encourage dramatic writing. Play music whilst students are writing. After this, ask students to swap their stories and encourage students to read out whenever they see an example of powerful writing, even if it is only a phrase or a sentence. This is genuine praise and affirmation.

Activity 5: Taking Stock on the Island

Teacher sets the scene. Lush tropical island, well wooded with streams. Coral reef full of fish, BUT, there is smoke coming from the hills, there are sounds of growling and soon, the survivors find foot-marks near-by. After some exhausted sleep, the 24 survivors look around and then decide to take stock of their situation.

 SWOT Analysis (A3 sheets)

Activity 6: Develop the Map

 Each team is given an A3 sized map of the island. (See the Power Point at my web site). Teacher to explain the features. Each team is to decide where to establish their camp/fort in the most strategic position from a defensive point of view. Each team can add 4 features to the island, such as a fresh water lake. These 4 features must be added to the map and labelled. Ask each team to report back, explaining why they have positioned their camp/fort in a particular position.

Activity 7: Design Your Community with Fortification

(showing all details including position, size in metres, height, and clear area in front of fort, housing, water collection and storage. Also design some defensive apparatus from local and personal resources.) All features must be labelled.

 Use **Mind Maps** and **Six Hats** as well as all the materials brought from the ship, the materials in the life boats and the natural resources of the island

Each team is supplied with A3 paper or larger and textas. Label the plan.

Self assess each team's plan by use of **Pros:Cons:Improve** or **Yellow Hat**, **Black Hat** and **Green Hat**.

Activity 8: Peer Assessment

Each team swaps their plans with another team, also supplying one team member to act as an explainer. The job of each team is to assess the work of the other team and offer feedback.

HOW ➡ **Pros:Cons:Improve** or **Yellow, Black** and **Green Hats**.

Return assessment and materials to home teams. Home teams decide whether or not to revise and improve their plans.

Each team then reports back to whole group.

Activity 9: Designing a Set of Community Rules

Each team is to design a set of community rules for daily living and peaceful co-existence with the aim of avoiding turmoil.

HOW ➡ Students are asked to list all the problems associated with society today in Australia and elsewhere. They use a **Noisy Round Robin** between the four groups. They then categorize and classify the ideas and categories are listed on the whiteboard for all to see. Students discuss in their teams the various problems and develop a set of ten rules for community living on the island, this time using a **1:4: P: C: R**.

Activity 10: Assessing the Sets of Rules for Community Living

Note that the teacher needs to select two or three sets of rules (it would be tedious to assess all eight sets of rules)

HOW ➡ **Decision Making Matrix** (**DMM**). Teacher to explain the **DMM** and start to assess the four sets of rules using the **DMM** at the whiteboard. Each group then completes the **DMM** and reports back.

Note that the four sets need to be photocopied so that each team has a full set of the rules.

Activity 11: Creating a Story About Survival on the Island

HOW ➡ **Word Association and Launch Pad**. Teacher models this first at the board and each individual student (or pairs of students) completes their own **Word Association** and uses this as well as all other materials produced to write their story of survival on the island.

Note that the teacher can add other complications such as planes flying past, human skeleton being found, man traps being discovered etc. in order to offer students greater opportunities for creative story telling.

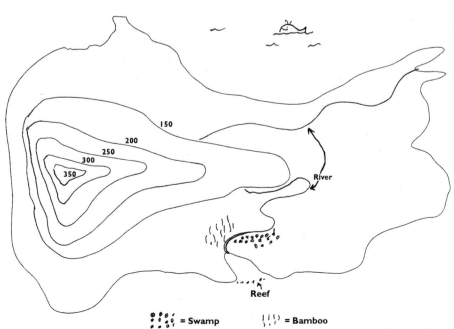

Topographical Map of the Island

Ⓟ

'The Island' from the Bonus Lesson Plan – 'Island Survival' (p111–113)

Ⓟ

'The Sinking Ship' from the Bonus Lesson Plan – 'Island Survival' (p111–113)

Please note: for ease of photocopying/scanning, larger illustrations for the lesson plan 'Island Survival', are provided above and on pages 117, 124 and 125.

Generic Sequence for any Design Project

This is a very generic and basic sequence for any design project and can be completed in 3–4 classroom lessons of 50 minutes each but can also be employed over a period of 4–6 weeks, with additional activities, teacher input and research. You will notice the use of specific thinking tools to enhance student engagement, ownership and motivation.

Context: An Advertising Project (Class of 30 students)

Step 1   Teacher presents ten different advertisements, taken from newspapers, magazines, brochures, etc. Each group of three students receives one advert which has a blank sheet attached. Their task is to list ALL the features of each advert.

 Hot Potato (p.84) Each group has 90 seconds to study the advert, discuss and list any feature (eg, different size font, different colours, suggested benefits, money details etc). After 90 seconds, the teacher says "Yoplait" (remember that this is French for 'pass the paper to the next table!!') and each group now has a new advert, studies this and adds any feature not already mentioned by the previous group. The swapping continues until all groups have seen each advert or until the teacher feels that there are no more features to add. (Remember, Understand and Analyse)

The teacher can ask for major features and add a few of her/his own. A comprehensive list can now be made.

Step 2   Teacher input on advertising. Note taking by students. Add features to the comprehensive list from Step 1. Additional activity could be to categorise the various components of advertisements. (Remember, Understand and Apply)

Step 3   Practise designing an advertisement.

Teacher suggests a topic or asks students for a topic, then:

  a) completes a **Y Chart** (p.47) with the class on white board (An)

b) each group of four students adds to that **Y Chart**, so that each group is somewhat different. (An)

c) students use the **1:4:P:C:R** strategy (p.92) to design an advert for that topic. Note that students must be encouraged to use the ideas generated in the **Y Chart**. (Create). Teacher debriefs the final six or seven products in terms of all the features listed in Step 1 and the teacher input in Step 2. (Apply)

Step 4   Teacher presents two professionally produced adverts (possibly a copy of each advert for each group of four students) and asks the simple question, "Which advertisement is more effective?"

 Decision Making Matrix (p.67)

Criteria Value ↓ (1-5)	1 Colour	2	3	4	5	6	7	8	Total
Advert A									
Advert B									

Step 5   Design your own advertisement for a topic of issue of your choice.

1. Each student selects a topic or subject of their choice.

 2. Each students completes a **Y Chart** (p.47) on that topic to flesh it out.

3. Each student begins to design their own advertisement, using the ideas from Steps 1 and 2 and from their **Y Chart**. Note that students must be sure to include the criteria listed in the **DMM** in Step 4 since these criteria were understood to be important in determining which advert was more effective.

Note that the advertisement could be a poster, a brochure, an email flier, a 30 second TV advert or the form of any type of advertisement in use by the industry.

Wall Posters

You may consider enlarging, colouring and laminating some of these posters and displaying these on your classroom walls if they suit the message you are attempting to promote with your students.

Explanation of each poster

Only *(p.118)*

I discourage students from using the word **ONLY** in the context of placing a value on their actions. The reason is that most of the time, people are trying their best and by using this word, they are assigning a lesser or diminished value to themselves. It is a fairly negative word and used regularly could lead to an incremental diminution of self-worth. Take the following examples:

- I **only** came third
- I am **only** in the B team
- I am **only** vice captain
- I am **only** a boy
- I am **only** a girl.

It gets worse. How about:
- I am **only** a classroom teacher
- I am **only** a mother or house wife
- I am **only** a deputy principal.

The point is that we are not *only*, we are *we*. In a healthy democracy, there ought to be a heightened sense of self-worth and a belief in the dignity of each type of work , profession, pursuit and involvement. Our students will perform better with a good self-image and as teachers we play a huge role in promoting that self-image.

Another diminishing word is **JUST**. Both of these words tend to offer excuses for mediocre performances in school and promote the Pygmalion principle of self-fulfilling prophesy.

I Can't + OO *(p.118)*

A simple device to remind students to be more positive. This then becomes a stock class response to a student who says "**I Can't**". The response is "**Add OO**" so that the "I can't" becomes "**I can too**".

Yet *(p.119)*

Similar to **I Can't + OO**. I first heard this some years ago from a group of teachers in West Australia. Too often learners use the term "I can't do ..." and take on a pessimistic and negative attitude. The truth is that given the will to learn, assisted by a dedicated teacher and given time and the right learning style, most students can learn anything. Teachers need to point out the negative self-talk and encourage students to be aware of this negative self talk and then add the word "**YET**". Done regularly in the classroom, students soon get the message that they are in the presence of a teacher who believes in them and who wants positive self-talk in the classroom.

One point to note is that I am quite content to be a hypocrite and not change the sentence "I cannot bungy-jump!"

OIE-ETCCC *(p.119)*

This is one of the mottos for the various Rodin Enrichment Programs we run during the holidays. It is very easy for all of us to perform in an ordinary manner as teachers, students, on the sports field, as parents, friends and colleagues. However, when we inject our true personality, creativity, risk-taking ability into what we do, we are more likely to perform out of or beyond the ordinary. This is surely the goal of all places of learning and growth and so I encourage my students to go for the **ETCCC** attitude.

I normally follow this with some information on left and right brain types of thinking allied to a few lateral problem solving puzzles as explained on page 79.

If You Always Do What You Always Did, You'll Always Get What You Always Got... *(p.73)*

One of the great dangers for teachers is substantially repeating each year. This results in boredom and desensitised creativity. The same problem exists for students. We can inspire ourselves and our students by encouraging **different routes** and **ways** of doing something.

If it Ain't Broke, Don't Fix it and How Could It Be Even Better *(p.120)*

Not bad advice but it can also be **dangerous**. It is both an invitation to **complacency** and a **barrier to creativity**. The real question for the thinking classroom is even though it may not be broke, **could it be 'even' better**?

Good thinkers attempt to be proactive. In other words, they refuse to be seduced by success and refuse to rest on their laurels. Instead they regularly reflect on their personal practice to ask how they can **improve** that which is **already good**.

Comfort Zone *(p.121)*

Too often we ascribe a negative paradigm to the idea of being forced out of '**our comfort zone**'. I wonder if we would have more people volunteering for new experiences if we changed our terminology and instead invited people to "**move into their growth zone**" or "**move into their excitement zone**".

Bloom's Taxonomy *(p.122)*

Each of the icons related to the six levels of Bloom's Taxonomy are very clear. If students are taught the language of Bloom's, it is more likely that they will be more focused and more successful. (See p.85.)

To remove any uncertainty, I explain to students that the **Analysis** is like a checker board with each square containing information on a subtopic of the object of study. **Synthesis** is like four lightning bolts (from **Knowledge** through to **Analysis** thinking) creating a partially or totally new idea or product. **Evaluation** is to do with decision making – like a judge.

The information in brackets (see p.122) reflects the changes suggested by the review of Bloom's Taxonomy by Lorin Anderson, and a team of cognitive psychologists. Apart from changing the words, the other shift is from nouns to verbs as well as elevating **Create** above **Evaluate**.

'In the Torpedo's Sights' from the Bonus Lesson Plan 'Island Survival' (p111–113)

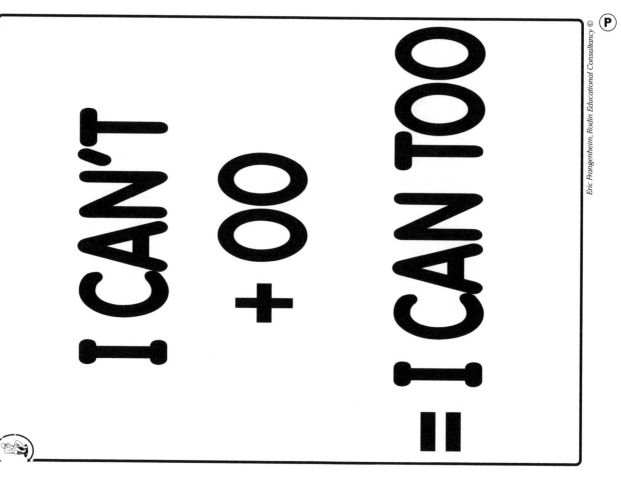

I CAN'T
+ OO
= I CAN TOO

ONLY

You are NOT ONLY
You are YOU

A Mind Set

OIE–ETCCC

Ordinary is Easy –

Extraordinary Takes

- ### Creativity
- ### Courage
- ### Commitment

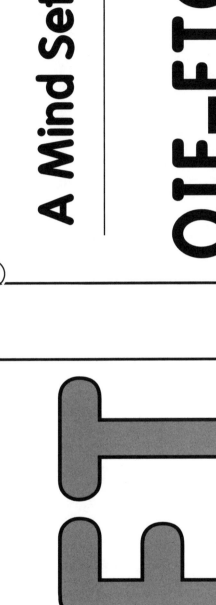

YET

the strongest
word in
LEARNING

It may not
be broken

BUT

How could it be

EVEN

BETTER?

If it ain't
BROKE

Don't Fix it!!

An invitation for
COMPLACENCY?

A barrier to
CREATIVITY?

Ⓟ

Paradigm Shift

Out of My "Comfort Zone"

OR

- ## Into My "Growth Zone"

- ## Into My "Excitement Zone"

Eric Frangenheim, Rodin Educational Consultancy ©

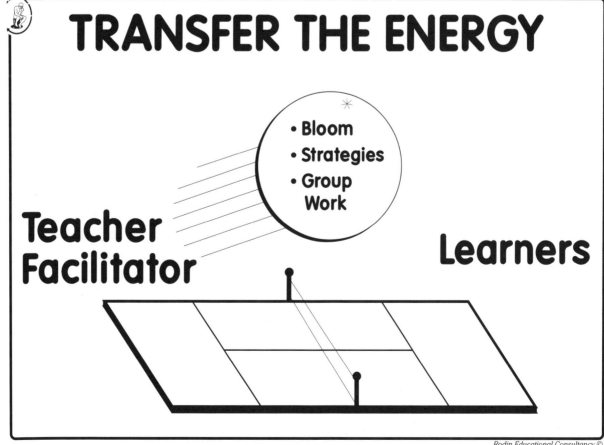

TRANSFER THE ENERGY

- **Bloom**
- **Strategies**
- **Group Work**

Teacher Facilitator

Learners

Rodin Educational Consultancy ©

Bloom's Taxonomy

# CREATE **(Synthesis)**	
# EVALUATE **(Evaluation)**	
# ANALYSE **(Analysis)**	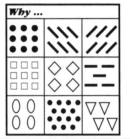
# APPLY **(Application)**	
# UNDERSTAND **(Comprehension)**	
# REMEMBER **(Knowledge)**	

Eric Frangenheim, Rodin Educational Consultancy ©

Wall Posters Index

Templates

References

Armstrong, Thomas. ***Multiple Intelligences in the Thinking Classroom.*** ASCD, Virginia. (1994)

Aronson, E. ***The Jigsaw Classroom***. Sage Publications, Beverly Hills, CA.

Covey, Stephen R. ***The 7 Habits of Highly Effective Families***, Allen & Unwin, NSW (1997)

Dalton, J. ***Adventures in Thinking***. Thomas Nelson Australia. (1985)

Eberle, Bob. ***Scamper***. D.O.K. Publisher. Reprinted 1991, Hawker Brownlow, Melbourne. (1987)

Kagan, Dr Spencer. ***Cooperative Learning***. Kagan Cooperative Learning, San Juan, CA. (1994)

Langrehr, J. ***Teach Thinking Strategies***. Longman Chesshire, Melbourne. (1990)

McCarthy, Kevin W. ***The On-Purpose Person (Making Your Life Make Sense)***, Pinon Press Colorado Springs (1992)

Ryan, Tony. ***Thinkers Keys CD***, Thinkers Keys Pty. Ltd. (2005) (www.thinkerskeys.com)

Sloan, P. ***Lateral Thinking Puzzlers***. Sterling Publishing Co., Inc, New York. (1992)

'The Lifeboat Journey' from the Bonus Lesson Plan 'Island Survival' (p111–113)

'Fishing, BUT...' from the Bonus Lesson Plan 'Island Survival' (p111–113)

Notes

'The Camp' from the Bonus Lesson Plan 'Island Survival' (p111–113)

About the Author

Eric has lived in Indonesia, Malaysia, Holland, Kenya, Zimbabwe and South Africa, and is now a citizen of Australia. He was trained as a high school history teacher and since 1970 has taught in Zimbabwe, South Africa and Queensland. He has held the positions of Subject Master, Head of Department and Deputy Principal. After eighteen months as a teacher in Rockhampton, he was appointed as Education Adviser for Gifted and Talented Students in the Capricornia Region with the Queensland Department of Education for four years. He then coordinated the Gifted and Talented program at an independent school in Brisbane for three years.

Since December 1995, Eric has been an independent education consultant and is the director of Rodin Educational Consultancy. His major focus is the infusion of thinking strategies into the daily curriculum, providing not only for the potentially more able, but also for all students. This book is aimed at promoting the use of thinking and learning strategies in classrooms and in professional development workshops. His second book, *'The Reconciliation of Goldilocks and the Three Bears'* (March 1999), is aimed at primary school teachers. The book consists of the story of the sequel, a unit plan, strategies guide and extension materials.

Since 2001, he has promoted The Xpata Lesson Planner, an on-line tool for teachers, developed with Tony Ryan. He is also the co-creator of the Innovative Teachers' Companion (a teacher resource diary) with Gerard Alford and Paul Herbert.

Rodin Educational Consultancy

Telephone: 61 7 3287 6633

Fax: 61 7 3287 6755

e-mail: ericf@rodineducation.com.au

Web page: www.rodineducation.com.au (See 'Range of Services')

The Xpata Lesson Planner: www.xpata.com

The Innovative Teachers' Companion: www.itcpublications.com.au

Offering Schools
- Teacher Inservice Workshops
- Demonstration lessons
- Lesson Brush Unit Planning
- Unit and Work Program modification in terms of thinking strategies
- Simulated Balance of Power Game

Offering Workshops in learning and teaching

Rodin Educational Consultancy networks with other presenters/consultants in the areas of:
- Learning/Human Potential
- Computers
- English
- Science
- Teaching and Learning (Primary)